DODGE

IN THE

HALL OF FAME

Ebbets Field served as a rallying point for the many diverse neighborhoods of Brooklyn. Rev. Gardner Taylor spoke of serving in Brooklyn in the days of Jackie Robinson: "Brooklyn became a symbol of hope and freedom and deliverance." Immigrants from all over the world, "Shanghai, Italy, Russia, Austria . . . Irish . . . and Blacks came from the south forming a mosaic of tight-knit communities. . . . Tribes isolated among themselves . . . they gathered at Ebbets Field." A temple of and for baseball. (Courtesy of David Hickey.)

FRONT COVER: In the June 1965 issue of *Baseball Digest*, Jackie Robinson reflected upon his election to the hall of fame. "If this can happen to a guy whose parents were virtually slaves, a guy from a broken home, a guy whose mother worked as a domestic from sun up to sun down; if this can happen to someone who in his early years who was a delinquent . . . then it can happen to you kids out there who think that life is against you." (Courtesy of the National Baseball Hall of Fame.)

COVER BACKGROUND: Dodger manager Leo Durocher arrives, shirtless on a horse-drawn wagon, at Doubleday Field for the 1943 hall of fame game versus the White Sox. Four thousand gathered to witness the fourth annual hall of fame game. Before the game, Dodger Paul Waner won a golf tournament using only a nine iron and putter, the only two left-handed golf clubs to be found in Cooperstown. (Courtesy of David Hickey.)

BACK COVER: On June 4, 1972, in a pregame ceremony at Dodger Stadium, the numbers of Jackie Robinson (No. 42), Roy Campanella (No. 39), and Sandy Koufax (No. 32) were retired, the first Brooklyn/Los Angeles Dodger numbers to be so honored. In 1997, Robinson's No. 42 was retired in perpetuity throughout all of Major League Baseball (MLB). Players wearing No. 42 at that time were allowed to continue wearing it, with Mariano Rivera being the last to do so. (Courtesy of David Hickey.)

DODGERS
IN THE
HALL OF FAME

Raymond Sinibaldi, Kerry Keene, and David Hickey

ARCADIA
PUBLISHING

Copyright © 2023 by Raymond Sinibaldi, Kerry Keene, and David Hickey
ISBN 978-1-4671-0994-9

Published by Arcadia Publishing
Charleston, South Carolina

Printed in the United States of America

Library of Congress Control Number: 2023934472

For all general information, please contact Arcadia Publishing:
Telephone 843-853-2070
Fax 843-853-0044
E-mail sales@arcadiapublishing.com
For customer service and orders:
Toll-Free 1-888-313-2665

Visit us on the Internet at www.arcadiapublishing.com

For the Blackwoods, Michael, Cheryl, "Bigs," and Molly. Your love and light brighten the world. You will always be Christmas to me.

—Ray

To my dear late friend Steve Adamson, who as a young autograph collector personally got the signatures of Jackie Robinson and Roy Campanella at the entrance of a Boston hotel and proudly showed them to me decades later.

—Kerry

For my first grandchild Olivia May Kelly—follow your dreams, your world can be anything you want it to be. Love, Papa

—David

CONTENTS

Acknowledgments   6

Introduction   7

1.   From Brooklyn Grays to Dodger Blue   11

2.   Dem Hall of Fame Bums   41

3.   The Visionary   59

4.   Baseball in Black and White   65

5.   The Boys of Summer   79

6.   Goodbye, Flatbush; Hello, Hollywood   89

7.   The Left Arm of God   103

8.   Lasorda's Dodger Town   113

ACKNOWLEDGMENTS

The Society for American Baseball Research (SABR) bio project is a national baseball treasure, and baseballreference.com is a constant source of both information and amazement; both were an integral part of this story. Nothing brings a clearer perspective than to read about people and the events they create than to read about them as they happened; Newspapers.com allows that to happen, and for that, we are grateful. Quotes contained herein came from biographies, newspapers, magazines, and previously recorded interviews. The treasure trove that is the National Baseball Hall of Fame website contributed as well. To Caitrin Cunningham, Ryan Vied, and Erin Vosgien of Arcadia, working with you is not work. Thanks to Rachael Adams for her insights and, as always, Lynda—*sei la mia anima e i miei cuori ispirazione.*

All photographs of hall of fame plaques were taken by David Hickey.

Unless otherwise noted, all photographs in chapters one, six, and eight are from David Hickey's personal collection; chapters two and five are from Kerry Keene's personal collection; and chapters three, four, and seven are from Raymond Sinibaldi's personal collection. Library of Congress is abbreviated as "LOC" throughout.

On June 12, 1939, the baseball world gathered on the lawn outside the new National Baseball Hall of Fame in Cooperstown, New York. The classes of 1936, 1937, 1938, and 1939, comprising 25 men, were inducted. One of them was Wee Willie Keeler, the first member of the storied franchise of the Brooklyn/Los Angeles Dodgers to be so honored.

INTRODUCTION

Born in Brooklyn, New York, in 1883, they have been formally known as the Atlantics, the Grays, the Grooms, the Bridegrooms, the Superbas, and the Robins. Yet beginning in 1895, sportswriters and cranks (fans) often referred to them as "the Trolley Dodgers." It was a nickname born of a foreboding reality that became a part of life for Brooklynites—the inception of electric trolley cars. Navigating (dodging) their way around the trolley cars was often a matter of life and death. The Brooklyn Nine were simultaneously referred to by many different nicknames at the same time, often at the whim of whichever sports writer was writing whichever story. Some of the more colorful ones included "Dem Bums" and "the Church City Nine." In 1933, the word "Dodgers" appeared on their uniforms for the first time, and during the subsequent war years, the name "Trolley" disappeared from the lexicon of sportswriters and pundits.

After eight last name changes, the team changed its first name from "Brooklyn" to "Los Angeles" in 1958, when they, along with the New York Giants, headed west to California. A bold move that literally changed the landscape of Major League Baseball.

Joining the American Association in 1884, the brand-new Atlantics stumbled their way to ninth place in the 13-team league. Three pitchers handled the pitching through the 110-game schedule. They competed in the American Association through the 1889 season, calling themselves the Grays and then the Bridegrooms. In 1890, they joined the eight-team National League and went on to capture their first pennant, taking on the Louisville Colonels of the American Association in the World Series. The series was tied three games apiece following a Colonels 8-2 win on a raw late October day. The *New York Times* wrote, "It was decided to postpone the two remaining games to the spring . . . this was done on account of the disagreeable state of the weather for ball playing." The outcome was never decided.

The 1891 season brought the first future hall of famer to Brooklyn when player/manager John Montgomery Ward joined the Bridegrooms; the name derived from the fact that in 1888 no less than six of the players exchanged nuptials. Ward added Dan Brouthers to the roster in 1892 and Tommy McCarthy in 1896. When Ned Hanlon arrived from Baltimore in 1899, he brought with him "Wee Willie" Keeler, Joe Kelley, and Hughie Jennings. The arrival of Hanlon prompted the scribes to assign a new moniker to the Brooklyn baseball entity, "the Superbas" (Latin for "superb"). This name came from a vaudeville act owned by three Hanlon brothers (no relation) called the "Hanlons' Superba." An "Iron Man" was added to the Superbas in 1900, rounding out the eight 19th-century Dodgers who would one day enter Cooperstown's hall of immortality.

From 1884 through 1912, the Dodgers played in four different stadiums in the borough of Brooklyn. On March 4, 1912, a groundbreaking ceremony was held near "Pig Town" in the Flatbush neighborhood of Brooklyn. The *New York Evening World* reported, "President Charley H. Ebbets . . . shoved a solid silver . . . spade into the ground six feet from the curb on Bedford Avenue, between Sullivan and Montgomery streets . . . tossed a lump of clay into the air; and thus started the work of construction of 'Ebbets Field', the new baseball home of the Trolley Dodgers." With none other than Thomas Edison lending his brain to the ballpark construction and surviving a steelworkers' strike, the Trolley Dodgers opened the 1913 season in Ebbets Field. In 1914, Wilbert "Uncle Robbie" Robinson was placed at the helm of a team that had not achieved 70 wins in more than a decade. He restored respectability, and scribes began referring to the Brooklyn team as the Robins. Robinson managed for 18 seasons in Brooklyn and was the skipper when the word "Dodgers" appeared on the team's jersey for the first time. Following his departure, the Dodgers suffered five consecutive losing seasons under three different managers. One of them was Charles Dillon Stengel, who had come up through the Brooklyn system and played under Robinson for four seasons. Both reached Cooperstown's hallowed halls: Robinson in 1945 and Stengel in 1966.

In June 1938, on the very same night that Johnny Vander Meer attempted to throw his third straight no-hitter, Babe Ruth appeared in the Brooklyn Dodger's first base coaching box at Ebbets Field. In his 1974 biography *Babe: The Legend Comes to Life*, author Robert Creamer explained how it came to be. "Vander Meer's feat was front-page news, but earlier in the evening the biggest excitement in the ballpark was the arrival of Babe. . . . A stir ran through the crowd and fans swarmed around him. Larry McPhail, who had become executive vice-president of the Dodgers, was doing everything he could to pump life into this moribund franchise. He remembered the Babe Ruth Day he had put on in Cincinnati three years earlier, and the crowd the Babe attracted." In a matter of days, Babe was wearing the uniform of the "Flatbushers" and coaching first base. The Brooklyn Dodger uniform was the last Major League Baseball (MLB) uniform worn, in an official capacity, by "the Sultan of Swat." His tenure as a Dodger ended with the 1938 season.

America stood on the precipice of war in 1940 when the Dodgers acquired a 19-year-old shortstop from the Boston Red Sox. Within months after the bombing of Pearl Harbor, history's architect arrived at the scene. Harold "Pee Wee" Reese and Wesley Branch Rickey would both play significant roles in events that would transcend baseball and transform America.

In 1947, Jack Roosevelt Robinson took the field for the Brooklyn Dodgers, igniting a movement that would change baseball, the country, and the world forever.

The Dodgers became the second team to travel out of the country for spring training, choosing to prepare for the 1942 season in Havana, Cuba. They returned to Cuba in 1947 and constructed Dodgertown in 1948, all to avoid the scourge of the segregated South during spring training and to ease the burden for Robinson, Roy Campanella, and the Dodgers of color to follow.

The decade of the 1950s brought six future hall of famers to Brooklyn, five of whom played a highly significant role in transforming the Dodgers and baseball. In October 1950, Walter O'Malley, who had been an executive and partial owner since 1942, became the principal owner. The Dodgers finished tied for first with the Giants in 1951, only to lose to Bobby Thomson's "shot heard round the world." They won the pennant in both 1952 and 1953 only to fall to the Yankees twice in the World Series. The 1953 team won 105 games, a team record that stood until 2019, and in 1954, O'Malley turned to a homegrown Dodger to skipper his club.

Walter Alston took the helm, beginning a stretch of 42 years that would see only two men manage the Dodgers. Both ended up in the hall of fame, and both made their Dodger debut in the same year. In August 1954, rookie manager Alston called up a 26-year-old lefty whom he had managed in Montreal—his name, Tommy Lasorda. On August 27, 1955, nineteen-year-old Sanford Koufax made his second big-league start, shutting out the Cincinnati Reds. Thirty-eight days later, the Brooklyn Dodgers won their first World Series. Twenty-year-old Don Drysdale followed him to Brooklyn the following year and, in 1957, emerged as the ace of the staff.

Branch Rickey departed Brooklyn in 1950. Walter O'Malley grabbed the reins, and by the end of the decade, the franchise owned their own plane, won four pennants and a World Series in Brooklyn, and in 1959, the Los Angeles Dodgers captured their first pennant and World Series..

The new decade dawned with Sandy Koufax on the doorstep of becoming one of baseball's most dominant pitchers of all time. As he emerged, Dodger dominance emerged with him. Alston's crew finished tied with the Giants in 1962, only to lose again in a playoff, as they had done a decade earlier. As Sandy Koufax created a new paradigm for pitchers, Alston rode his "Left arm of God" to three pennants, capturing the World Series in 1963 and 1965. Don Sutton arrived in 1966 and became the Dodgers' first hall of famer to begin his career in Los Angeles.

Some aging hall of famers made their way through Los Angeles in the early 1970s. Frank Robinson came on board for the 1972 season, and in 1975, former Giant great Juan Marichal donned Dodger blue. In 14 seasons with San Francisco, the "Dominican Dandy" pitched 476 innings against his arch rival. He came to Los Angeles to right a wrong. The boys in blue garnered one more pennant for their aging skipper in 1974, and with four games remaining in the 1976 season, Walter Alston turned the managerial reins over to Tommy Lasorda.

For two decades, Lasorda piloted the Dodgers, winning four NL pennants and two World Series while reaching the postseason playoffs seven times. Under Lasorda, two players took their first steps toward Cooperstown wearing a Dodger uniform. Both Pedro Martinez and Mike Piazza made their major-league debuts in September 1992, twenty-three days apart.

The new millennium dawned ushering in an unmatched era of regular season success for the storied Dodger franchise, and two of baseball's truly elite players made their way to Los Angeles in their waning days. All-time leading base stealer Rickey Henderson stole his last base in Dodger Stadium in 2003, and in 2008, Greg Maddux earned the last of his 355 wins as a Dodger. Joe Torre also ended his career in the Golden State, managing from 2008 to 2010, and in 2014, he became the 10th Dodger skipper to be enshrined in Cooperstown.

A century removed from the Brooklyn Robins' loss to the Cleveland Indians in the 1920 World Series, the Los Angeles Dodgers captured their seventh world championship. Asterisks cannot help but be attached to this season simply because baseball fans a century hence will want to know why only 60 games were played. That notwithstanding, the 2020 world championship was sandwiched between two 106-win seasons. As the 2023 season begins, they are in the midst of their greatest decade. Five years of 90-plus wins, and four years of 100-plus wins, including an astounding 111 games in 2022. In the abbreviated 2020 world championship year, their winning percentage was .717. Two of the game's finest gentlemen are the Dodgers' latest hall of fame inductees. In 2022, a half-century after he passed, Gil Hodges finally joined his fellow "Boys of Summer" in the hall of fame, and in July 2023, Fred McGriff, a unanimous selection of the hall of fame's Contemporary Era Committee, found his way to bronzed immortality.

This is the story of all those who have worn Dodger blue and now eternally live among the pantheon of baseball's elite within the hallowed halls of the National Baseball Hall of Fame in Cooperstown, New York.

Construction on Dodger Stadium began in 1959, and in 1962, the Dodgers moved in. The cost was $23 million ($206 million in 2020). The first five years in their new home brought three NL pennants and two World Series. From 1962 through 2022, the stadium hosted two MLB All-Star Games, 10 World Series, 13 no-hitters, and the 1984 Olympics, and 11 retired numbers of Dodger greats adorn the facade. It has the largest seating capacity in Major League Baseball, and it is the third-oldest ballpark in the game.

Once voted by fans as the Dodgers "most memorable personality," Vin Scully received the hall of fame's Ford Frick Award in 1982. The voice of the Dodgers for 67 years, he truly was the bridge between Brooklyn and Los Angeles, witnessing the hall of fame careers of dozens of Dodgers. Not too bad for a "red-haired kid with a hole in his pants and his shirt-tail hangin' out," who played "stickball in the streets of New York," Scully opined in 1982.

FROM BROOKLYN GRAYS TO DODGER BLUE

In June 1884, Moses Fleetwood Walker visited Brooklyn with Toledo, playing two games with the Blue Stockings. The *Brooklyn Union* reported that "Walker, the colored catcher of the Toledos, proved himself very efficient." The following day, Walker became the first Black major-league player to record a base hit in the borough of Brooklyn. It would be 22,947 days before Jackie Robinson would duplicate that feat.

History states that the Brooklyn baseball entity was called the Grays from 1885 through 1887. However, the only mention newspapers of the time make to the Brooklyn Grays references military regiments. The Bridegrooms (or just "Grooms") and Ned Hanlon's Superbas quickly followed.

On April 26, 1895, the Brooklyn baseball team traveled to Baltimore to play the Orioles in a three-game series. "Brooklyn players are now known as Trolley Dodgers," wrote the *Times Union*, and the Dodgers were born. Behind the plate that day for the Orioles was a 31-year-old catcher named Wilbert Robinson, who would add his name to the Brooklyn team when he reported to the new Ebbets Field as their new manager in 1914.

In these early days of baseball, most teams had more than one nickname, and every so often, a list of them would appear in local newspapers. In 1899, "the Brooklyns" were referred to as "the Trolley-Dodgers," "the Bridegrooms," or "the Superbas." All true, but they were called the Grooms and just the Dodgers as well. When Wilbert Robinson came on board, the moniker of "Robins" was added to the list, an abbreviated version of "Uncle Robbie's Robins." The Bridegrooms was the first to fall by the wayside, and from 1915 through 1932, Robins and Dodgers were most commonly used, with Trolley Dodgers sprinkled throughout. Through the first three decades of the 20th century, any one or all of these nicknames were used and often within the same newspaper story. The word "Dodgers" appeared on their uniform for the first time in 1933, yet the other sobriquets would linger through the war years.

Whether they be Grays or not, Bridegrooms or Grooms, Superbas or Robins, Trolley Dodgers or just plain Dodgers, the fact remains that 22 men who wore the Brooklyn gray or Dodger blue through 1933 are enshrined in the National Baseball Hall of Fame.

JOHN MONTGOMERY WARD
1878 — 1894
PITCHING PIONEER WHO WON 158,
LOST 102 GAMES IN SEVEN YEARS.
PITCHED PERFECT GAME FOR PROVIDENCE
OF N.L. IN 1880.
TURNED TO SHORTSTOP AND MADE 2,151 HITS.
MANAGED NEW YORK AND BROOKLYN IN N.L.
PRESIDENT OF BOSTON, N.L. 1911-1912.
PLAYED IMPORTANT PART IN ESTABLISHING
MODERN ORGANIZED BASEBALL.

Debuting in 1878, John Montgomery "Monte" Ward went on to become one of 19th-century baseball's most influential figures. An outstanding pitcher early in his career, he won 47 games for Providence in 1879 and hurled the league's second perfect game the following year. An arm injury forced his conversion to the infield in 1884. Between baseball seasons, Ward earned a law degree from Columbia University and utilized his legal knowledge to pioneer the first players' union in 1885. Five years later, he was the driving force behind creating the rival Players League, which was run by players who were dissatisfied with their treatment from the National League owners. Ward served as the player/manager for the Brooklyn entry; however, the league folded after one season. Ward then joined the National League Brooklyn team as its player/manager in 1891 and 1892 and later served as president of the Boston Braves. He was elected in 1964.

"Big Dan" Brouthers brought his considerable batting talents to Brooklyn in 1892 after 13 seasons as one of baseball's most powerful sluggers. Large for his era, the six-foot, two-inch, 207-pound Brouthers took over his usual first base position for manager John Ward. He arrived having already won four batting titles, and he had led his league in the on-base plus slugging (OPS) statistic seven times. He was elected in 1945.

DAN BROUTHERS

HARD-HITTING FIRST BASEMAN OF EIGHT MAJOR LEAGUE CLUBS, HE WAS PART OF ORIGINAL "BIG FOUR" OF BUFFALO. TRADED WITH OTHER MEMBERS OF THAT COMBINATION TO DETROIT, HE HIT .419 AS CITY WON ITS ONLY NATIONAL LEAGUE CHAMPIONSHIP IN 1887.

Although 34 years old, "old" for an athlete in the 1890s, Brouthers did not disappoint, providing Brooklyn with a highly productive season. He captured yet another batting title while also leading the league in hits, runs batted in, OPS, and total bases. In 1893, his final season with Brooklyn, he played just over half of the team's games but still managed a .337 batting average. Big Dan retired with a .342 career average.

THOMAS F. McCARTHY

ONE OF BOSTON'S "HEAVENLY TWINS" UNDER
MANAGER FRANK SELEE. OUTSTANDING BASE
RUNNER WHO STOLE 109 BASES FOR THE
BROWNS IN 1888. PIONEER IN TRAPPING FLY
BALLS IN THE OUTFIELD. HOLDS N.L. RECORD
FOR ASSISTS IN OUTFIELD-53 WITH BOSTON IN
1893. PLAYED 1268 GAMES IN MAJOR LEAGUES

Speedy outfielder Tommy McCarthy distinguished himself as an outstanding hitter, defensive player, base runner, and all-around talent. He is credited with helping create the hit-and-run play as well as the "trapped-ball" trick to catch base runners. While his career was rather short and his statistical record modest overall, historians have made the case that his election was based more on his on-field intelligence, strategic brilliance, and pioneering play. He was elected in 1946.

Listed among the league leaders in stolen bases and outfield assists numerous times, McCarthy contributed to three league pennants in St. Louis and Boston before signing with Brooklyn. The hope was he would assist Brooklyn in their pursuit of the 1896 pennant; however, the Grooms struggled, and he retired at season's end. McCarthy is the only hall of famer who played in the short-lived Union Association in 1884. He returned to Brooklyn as a coach in 1921.

Ned Hanlon, arguably the most accomplished manager of the 19th century, was initially ignored by the hall of fame and fell through the cracks of Cooperstown for six decades. After a noteworthy 13-year playing career, he embarked on a successful managerial career that included seven seasons at the helm in Brooklyn. The strategically brilliant Hanlon made a lasting name for himself leading the Orioles to the National League pennant each season from 1894 through 1896. In early 1899, Hanlon became Brooklyn's manager and was equally successful, leading the team to National League pennants in his first two seasons. Hanlon incorporated the regular use of the hit-and-run, sacrifice bunt, suicide squeeze, double steal, and the "Baltimore Chop." In 1937, the *Sporting News* deemed Hanlon to be the "game's greatest strategist" and "the Father of Modern Baseball." He was elected in 1996.

EDWARD HUGH HANLON
(NED)
PITTSBURGH, N.L. 1889, 1891
PITTSBURGH, P.L. 1890
BALTIMORE, N.L. 1892-1898
BROOKLYN, N.L. 1899-1905
CINCINNATI, N.L. 1906-1907
MANAGER OF FIVE PENNANT WINNING TEAMS WITH BALTIMORE
AND BROOKLYN, EMPLOYING INNOVATIVE TACTICS SUCH AS
HIT AND RUN, SQUEEZE AND "BALTIMORE CHOP". FOUR OF
HIS PLAYERS—McGRAW, ROBINSON, JENNINGS AND HUGGINS
THEMSELVES BECAME HALL OF FAME MANAGERS. ALSO HEADED
BASEBALL'S RULES COMMITTEE. A SPEEDY OUTFIELDER WITH
DETROIT DURING HIS PLAYING DAYS

The great Connie Mack once said, "I always rated Ned Hanlon as the greatest leader baseball ever had." In 1899, Hanlon came to a team that had not finished higher than fifth place in seven seasons. He took over a rebuilt roster that included several of his former Baltimore players and led the newly christened Superbas to a 101-47 record—a 47-game improvement over the previous season.

Willie Keeler returned to the place of his birth when he was purchased by his hometown Brooklyn Grooms in July 1893. The 21 year old played only 20 games with the Grooms and was traded to Baltimore after the season. Along with winning three National League championships (1894–1896), he had established himself as one of the top hitters of the decade. Keeler was elected in 1939.

WILLIE KEELER
"HIT 'EM WHERE THEY AINT!"
BASEBALL'S GREATEST PLACE-HITTER;
BEST BUNTER. BIG LEAGUE CAREER
1892 TO 1910 WITH N.Y. GIANTS,
BALTIMORE ORIOLES, BROOKLYN SUPERBAS,
N.Y. HIGHLANDERS. NATIONAL LEAGUE
BATTING CHAMPION '97-'98.

The diminutive Willie Keeler, who stood just five feet, four inches tall and weighed a mere 140 pounds, was one of the game's most effective hitters because of his ability to "hit 'em where they ain't." His 29-ounce, 30-inch bat is the smallest in major-league history, but with it, he displayed great bat control, place-hitting ability, and expert bunting, and he became known as the "King of the Place-Hitters." (Library of Congress.)

Willie Keeler's superior contact-hitting ability helped him record 206 singles in 1898, a record that stood for more than 100 years. After the joint Baltimore-Brooklyn ownership group transferred him back to the Superbas, Keeler, along with a few ex-Oriole teammates, helped lead Brooklyn to back-to-back championships in 1899 and 1900. He became the first person in franchise history to be enshrined in Cooperstown. In 1912, Keeler returned to Brooklyn as a coach (as seen here).

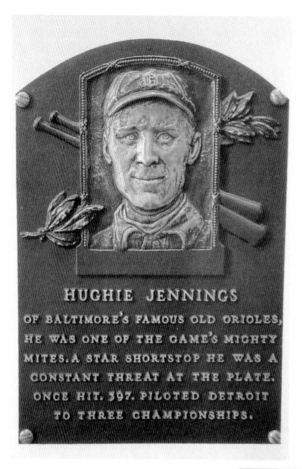

HUGHIE JENNINGS

OF BALTIMORE'S FAMOUS OLD ORIOLES, HE WAS ONE OF THE GAME'S MIGHTY MITES. A STAR SHORTSTOP HE WAS A CONSTANT THREAT AT THE PLATE. ONCE HIT .397. PILOTED DETROIT TO THREE CHAMPIONSHIPS.

Hughie Jennings was a star shortstop with the Orioles during their three consecutive pennant-winning seasons of 1894, 1895, and 1896. He was spectacular both defensively and offensively and recorded a .401 batting average in 1896. In 1899, he, like Keeler, was also transferred to Brooklyn to help the struggling team. He had suffered a serious arm injury the year before and thus played mainly at first base in Brooklyn. Jennings contributed to the team's considerable improvement, which yielded pennant-winning seasons in 1899 and 1900. He moved on to Philadelphia but returned briefly to Brooklyn in 1903. Jennings began a highly successful managerial career with Detroit, winning consecutive pennants in 1907, 1908, and 1909, his first three years at the helm. He was elected in 1945.

FROM BROOKLYN GRAYS TO DODGER BLUE

When left fielder Joe Kelley was transferred from the Orioles to Brooklyn for the 1899 campaign, the newly retooled Superbas were getting one of the finest all-around players of the decade. Legendary manager John McGraw, a teammate of Kelley with Baltimore, called him a "player with no prominent weakness." Kelley once had nine hits in nine at-bats during a doubleheader. He batted over .300 for 11 consecutive seasons and was perennially among the National League leaders in several hitting categories. Kelley served as team captain of the Orioles under manager Ned Hanlon, who also named him captain in Brooklyn. He provided yet another key cog in the Superbas' back-to-back championships of 1899 and 1900. In 1926, Kelley returned to Brooklyn as a coach. He was elected in 1971.

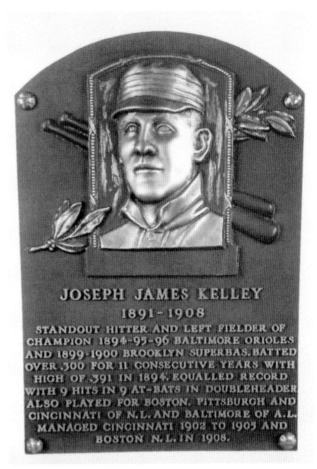

JOSEPH JAMES KELLEY
1891-1908
STANDOUT HITTER AND LEFT FIELDER OF CHAMPION 1894-95-96 BALTIMORE ORIOLES AND 1899-1900 BROOKLYN SUPERBAS. BATTED OVER .300 FOR 11 CONSECUTIVE YEARS WITH HIGH OF .391 IN 1894. EQUALLED RECORD WITH 9 HITS IN 9 AT-BATS IN DOUBLEHEADER ALSO PLAYED FOR BOSTON PITTSBURGH AND CINCINNATI OF N.L. AND BALTIMORE OF A.L. MANAGED CINCINNATI 1902 TO 1905 AND BOSTON N.L. IN 1908.

JOSEPH JEROME McGINNITY
"IRONMAN"
DISTINGUISHED AS THE PITCHER WHO HURLED
TWO GAMES ON ONE DAY THE MOST TIMES. DID
THIS ON FIVE OCCASIONS. WON BOTH GAMES
THREE TIMES. PLAYED WITH BALTIMORE,
BROOKLYN AND NEW YORK TEAMS IN N.L.
AND BALTIMORE IN A.L. GAINED MORE THAN
200 VICTORIES DURING CAREER. RECORDED
20 OR MORE VICTORIES SEVEN TIMES. IN TWO
SUCCESSIVE SEASONS WON AT LEAST 30 GAMES.

Joe McGinnity spent only one year in this storied organization, but it was a year for the ages. Unfortunately, it was the creation of the American League that prevented him from showcasing his talents in Brooklyn longer. Averaging 344 innings per season earned him the nickname "Iron Man." A 28-year-old rookie in 1899 with the Baltimore Orioles, he burst on the scene, leading the league with 28 wins. After the 1899 season, the NL trimmed from 12 teams to eight, with Baltimore and Brooklyn merging and continuing to call Flatbush home. Now pitching for the Superbas, McGinnity duplicated the feat and again led the league with 28 wins. In 1901, he followed former Baltimore teammates John McGraw and Wilbert Robinson to the newly created Orioles of the American League. He was elected in 1946.

Although he has slipped into obscurity in the century since he played, outfielder Zachariah Davis "Zack" Wheat is arguably the most accomplished Brooklyn player in the first 60 years of the franchise. In his 18 seasons (1909–1926), he set still-standing team records in games (2,322), hits (2,804), doubles (464), triples (171), at-bats (8,859), and total bases (4,003). At the time of his retirement following the 1927 season, only nine players in MLB's 50-plus-year history had recorded more than his 2,884 hits. Soft-spoken off the field, the left-handed hitting outfielder was immensely popular with the fans. An intense, fierce competitor on the field, hall-of-famer Buck O'Neill once said of him, "Zack Wheat was 165 pounds of scrap iron, rawhide, and guts." He was elected in 1959.

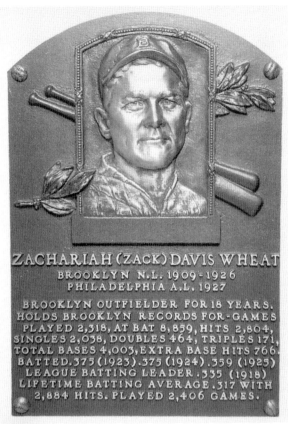

In 1915, the outfield wall at Ebbets Field featured the following advertisement for Tanglefoot Flypaper: "Wheat, Brooklyn, Caught 345 Flies. Tanglefoot caught 50,000,000,000." Zack Wheat led the National League in putouts again the following year, prompting *Baseball Magazine* to write in 1917, "What Nap Lajoie is to infielders, Zach Wheat is to outfielders, the finest mechanical craftsman of them all. . . . Wheat is the easiest, most graceful of outfielders with no close rivals."

Pictured are, from left to right, Brooklyn teammates Casey Stengel, Jimmy Johnston, Hi Myers, and Zack Wheat in 1916. The unique checkered pinstriped uniforms were worn only one season and abandoned the following year. Stengel, a teammate for six seasons, stated Wheat was "one of the grandest guys ever to wear a baseball uniform, one of the greatest batting teachers I have ever seen, one of the truest pals a man ever had, and one of the kindliest men God ever created." (George Bain Collection, LOC.)

Zach Wheat is pictured with his son Zachary on the dugout steps prior to a game at Ebbets Field in 1925. His Brooklyn uniform features a patch commemorating the National League's 50th season, and the black armband was in recognition of the death of team owner Charles Ebbets. Wheat's last home run at Ebbets Field was August 5, 1926, and it took him five minutes to hobble around the bases on one foot due to a charley horse.

In the years following the death of Zack Wheat on March 11, 1972, his former hometown of Polo, Missouri, placed a monument to him in the middle of a field on Main Street. An image of Wheat swinging a bat is on one side, and the opposite side references his farm having been located on the site, along with the text that appears on his hall of fame plaque.

WILBERT ROBINSON
"UNCLE ROBBIE"
STAR CATCHER FOR THE FAMOUS
BALTIMORE ORIOLES ON PENNANT CLUBS
OF 1894,'95 AND '96. HE LATER WON FAME
AS MANAGER OF THE BROOKLYN DODGERS
FROM 1914 THROUGH 1931. SET A RECORD OF
7 HITS IN 7 TIMES AT BAT IN SINGLE GAME.

Over the course of four decades, Wilbert Robinson distinguished himself as both a player and a manager. In the 1890s, he gained fame as the star catcher for the National League's Baltimore Orioles dynasty that won three straight pennants. His playing days ended in 1902, and he briefly managed Baltimore before leaving baseball for several years. In 1911, old friend and teammate John McGraw brought him in to serve as a Giants' coach, but he left after the two had a falling out following the 1913 World Series. Robinson accepted the Brooklyn managerial position and remained at the helm for 18 seasons (1914–1931). Uncle Robbie, as he came to be known, was a truly beloved figure in Flatbush and led the team to its first two pennants in the 20th century. He was elected in 1945. (Below, George Bain Collection, LOC.)

FROM BROOKLYN GRAYS TO DODGER BLUE

Manager Robinson (center) took on a tall task in 1914, leading a team that had not won more than 66 games or finished higher than fifth place since 1903. Progress was gradual, but Robinson guided them to 94 wins in 1916 and a long-awaited trip to the World Series. Unfortunately, the Robins "flock" lost to the Red Sox in five games. "Uncle Robbie" was the first purely 20th-century Dodger elected to the hall of fame.

After another World Series loss to Cleveland in 1920, Brooklyn kicked off a decade of futility. In 1925, after assuming the role of Dodger president while still field managing, Robinson's focus on the field declined, and the team's play became distracted and error-ridden. Known as "the Daffiness Boys," they are exemplified by one well-known incident in which three Robins base runners all occupied third base at the same time.

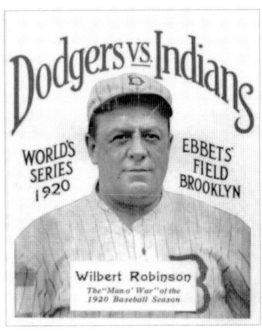

CHARLES DILLON STENGEL
"CASEY"

MANAGED NEW YORK YANKEES 1949-1960.
WON 10 PENNANTS AND 7 WORLD SERIES WITH
NEW YORK YANKEES. ONLY MANAGER TO WIN
5 CONSECUTIVE WORLD SERIES 1949-1953.
PLAYED OUTFIELD 1912-1925 WITH BROOKLYN,
PITTSBURGH, PHILADELPHIA, NEW YORK AND
BOSTON N.L. TEAMS. MANAGED BROOKLYN
1934-1936, BOSTON BRAVES 1938-1943,
NEW YORK METS 1962-1965.

Upon Charles Stengel's debut as Brooklyn's center fielder in late 1912, star left fielder Zack Wheat took him under his wing and gave him valuable guidance. Nicknamed "Casey" because he was a Kansas City (KC), Missouri, native, he quickly became known for his eccentricities and humorous language. Traded from Brooklyn to Pittsburgh in January 1918, he returned to Ebbets Field on June 6 and was loudly heckled by the crowd. Just before he went up to bat, Casey snuck a sparrow under his cap, and as he approached the batter's box, he politely took a bow, doffed his cap, and the bird flew out. It was Casey's imaginative way of "giving the crowd the bird." Following a stellar managerial career, including three seasons in Brooklyn, he was elected in 1966. (Below, George Bain Collection, LOC.)

FROM BROOKLYN GRAYS TO DODGER BLUE

Rube Marquard established himself as one of the finest left-handed pitchers of the "Dead Ball Era." His combined record of 73-28 contributed to three consecutive New York Giant pennants (1911–1913). Marquard made history by going 19-0 to start the 1912 campaign—still a record for the most wins without a loss to begin a season. Pitching for the Giants on April 15, 1915, he threw a no-hitter against Brooklyn, and six months later, the aging hurler was claimed off waivers by the Robins. In 1916, he finished second in the league in earned run average (ERA), helping Brooklyn reach the World Series. Marquard won 19 games in 1919 and again in his final Dodger season in 1920, helping them to another World Series appearance. Marquard was elected in 1971. (Below, George Bain Collection, LOC.)

RICHARD WILLIAM MARQUARD
"RUBE"
NEW YORK N.L., BROOKLYN N.L.,
CINCINNATI N.L., BOSTON N.L.,
1908–1925
THREE-TIME 20-GAME WINNER WITH
GIANT CHAMPIONS OF 1911-12-13. TIED ALL-TIME
RECORD WITH 19 VICTORIES IN A ROW WHILE
WINNING 26 AND LOSING 11 IN 1912. LED
N.L. IN WINNING PERCENTAGE AND
STRIKEOUTS IN 1911. TIED FOR MOST
VICTORIES, 1912. HURLED NO-HIT GAME
AGAINST DODGERS IN 1915.

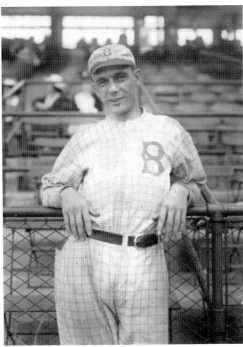

BURLEIGH ARLAND GRIMES
1916–1934

ONE OF THE GREAT SPITBALL PITCHERS.
WON 270 GAMES, LOST 212 FOR 7 MAJOR
LEAGUE CLUBS. FIVE 20 VICTORY SEASONS.
WON 13 IN ROW FOR GIANTS IN 1927.
MANAGED DODGERS IN 1937 AND 1938.
LIFETIME E.R.A. 3.52.

After watching a minor-league pitcher use it, teenager Burleigh Grimes became fascinated with the spitball. The young Grimes worked hard to master it, and by 1916, his hard work paid off, as he made his major-league debut with Pittsburgh. The spitball was ruled illegal in 1920; however, he was one of 17 practitioners grandfathered in and allowed to use it until retirement. Burleigh, who became the last pitcher to throw it legally in 1934, said, "I used to chew slippery elm—the bark, right off the tree. Come spring, the bark would get nice and loose, and you could slice it free without any trouble. What I cheeked was the fiber from inside, and that's what I put on the ball. The ball would break like hell, away from right-handers and in on lefties." Grimes was elected in 1964.

Burleigh Grimes had a reputation as an extremely fierce, intimidating, competitor, and he routinely featured the brushback pitch as part of his repertoire. Joining Brooklyn in 1918, he went on to be a mainstay of the pitching staff through 1926. His team, leading 23 victories in 1920, was his first of four 20-plus-win seasons with the Robins. Grimes, nicknamed "Ol' Stubblebeard," threw a 3-0 shutout against the Indians in the 1920 World Series.

When Grimes's 19-season pitching career concluded in 1934, he had notched 270 wins, with 269 of them in the National League. At the time, only two other 20th-century NL pitchers had more victories. The majority of Grimes's victories (158) came in a Brooklyn uniform. He returned to Ebbets Field to manage the Dodgers in 1937 and 1938, with Babe Ruth joining him as a coach in the final year.

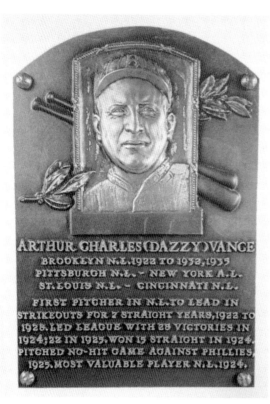

ARTHUR CHARLES (DAZZY) VANCE
BROOKLYN N.L. 1922 TO 1932, 1935
PITTSBURGH N.L. - NEW YORK A.L.
ST. LOUIS N.L. - CINCINNATI N.L.
FIRST PITCHER IN N.L. TO LEAD IN
STRIKEOUTS FOR 7 STRAIGHT YEARS, 1922 TO
1928. LED LEAGUE WITH 28 VICTORIES IN
1924; 22 IN 1925. WON 15 STRAIGHT IN 1924.
PITCHED NO-HIT GAME AGAINST PHILLIES,
1925. MOST VALUABLE PLAYER N.L. 1924.

Hard-throwing right-handed pitcher Arthur "Dazzy" Vance reached the age of 31 before winning his first major-league game. He had previously made a handful of appearances with Pittsburgh and the Yankees in 1915 and 1918 but had spent the vast majority of his pro career in the minor leagues. Vance had a recurring elbow problem that was remedied by a New Orleans doctor's surgery removing bone chips. He won 21 games in 1921 for the Pelicans, and Brooklyn purchased him just prior to the 1922 season. He was finally in the majors to stay. Nicknamed for his dazzling fastball, Dazzy had a very impressive rookie season, with the Robins winning 18 games, leading the league in shutouts, and starting a string of seven straight years, leading the league in strikeouts—the first pitcher to do so. Vance was elected in 1955.

Following his impressive rookie season, Dazzy Vance won 18 games for the second year in a row. He reached elite pitcher status in 1924, his best season, when he won the MVP award, for which the NL awarded him $1,000 in gold coins. Vance led the National League in wins (28), ERA (2.16), complete games (30), and strikeouts. On August 23, he struck out 15 Cubs, a new NL record for strikeouts in a nine-inning game.

In 1924, Dazzy Vance and teammate Burleigh Grimes finished one and two in strikeouts in the National League. It was only the second time in league history that teammates accomplished that feat. It would not happen again until Don Drysdale and Sandy Koufax did it in 1960. Vance learned of his election to the hall of fame when a Florida state trooper pulled his car over to tell him photographers were waiting for him at his house.

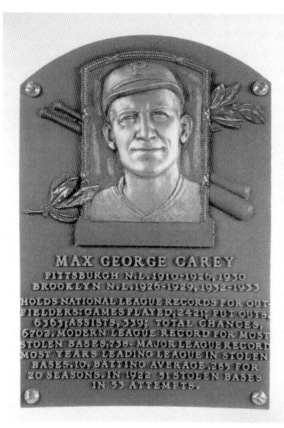

MAX GEORGE CAREY
PITTSBURGH N.L. 1910-1926, 1930
BROOKLYN N.L. 1926-1929, 1932-1933
HOLDS NATIONAL LEAGUE RECORDS FOR OUT-
FIELDERS: GAMES PLAYED, 2421; PUT OUTS,
6363; ASSISTS, 339; TOTAL CHANGES,
6702. MODERN LEAGUE RECORD FOR MOST
STOLEN BASES, 738. MAJOR LEAGUE RECORD
MOST YEARS LEADING LEAGUE IN STOLEN
BASES, 10, BATTING AVERAGE .285 FOR
20 SEASONS. IN 1922 51 STOLEN BASES
IN 53 ATTEMPTS.

"He was just as fast between the ears as he was with his feet," said sportswriter Joe Williams, and that is what made Max Carey "harder to stop than a run in a silk stocking." He led the National League in stolen bases 10 times, en route to 738 career steals, a record that stood until Lou Brock surpassed it in 1974. Defensively, his great speed helped him track down enough fly balls in the outfield to lead the league in putouts seven times. Carey had a spectacular World Series in 1925, batting .458 to help Pittsburgh capture a world championship. After a dispute with management the following August, he was placed on waivers, immediately claimed by the Robins, and spent his final few seasons in Brooklyn. Carey was elected in 1961.

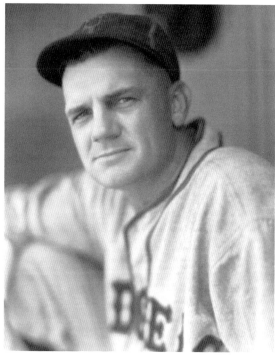

When longtime manager Wilbert Robinson retired in 1931, management brought back Max Carey to take over. Carey, pictured at center with players and fellow hall-of-famers Waite Hoyt (left) and Hack Wilson (right), led the team to 81 wins in 1932. After another disappointing season in 1933, he was replaced by coach Casey Stengel. In 1944, Carey managed the Milwaukee Chicks of the All-American Girls Professional Baseball League before serving as league president from 1945 to 1949.

Walter "Rabbit" Maranville was second in MVP voting in 1914 and finished in the top 10 four other times in his career. He was a big contributor to the "Miracle" Boston Braves' 1914 World Series upset over the heavily favored Philadelphia Athletics. He held the record for most seasons played (23) in the National League for more than 50 years until Pete Rose broke it in 1986. Maranville was inducted in 1954, just a few months after his death.

When Brooklyn acquired 14-year veteran shortstop Rabbit Maranville before the 1926 season, they were getting an extremely savvy defensive tactician who was essentially a manager on the field. The season before with the Chicago Cubs, he served as player/manager for 53 games. While only five foot, five inches, and 155 pounds, Rabbit was highly respected as a tough competitor. Maranville primarily played shortstop while with Brooklyn in 1926 before moving on to St. Louis in 1927.

By 1923, Dave Bancroft was regarded among the finest defensive shortstops in the National League and led his New York Giants to two World Series victories in four appearances. In 1922, he set a still-standing single-season record for chances by a shortstop with 1,046. His strategic intelligence and leadership skills prompted the Boston Braves to utilize him as a player/manager from 1924 to 1927. Bancroft was elected in 1971.

After the conclusion of the 1927 season, Dave Bancroft signed on with Brooklyn to play shortstop under longtime team manager Wilbert Robinson. He played in 149 of the Dodgers' 153 games during his first season, and while more of a defensive specialist, Bancroft did have four three-hit games that season. On opening day of 1929, he stroked four hits against his old Braves team, and in June, he had nine hits in 11 at-bats over three games.

ALFONSO RAMON LOPEZ

RENOWNED FOR SHREWD LEADERSHIP DURING 36-YEAR BIG LEAGUE CAREER AS CATCHER AND MANAGER. WON TWO PENNANTS AND HAD TEN SECOND-PLACE FINISHES WITH WINNING PCT. OF .581 IN 17 SEASONS AT HELM OF CLEVELAND AND CHICAGO WHITE SOX. ONLY MANAGER TO INTERRUPT YANKEES' PENNANT DYNASTY OF 1949-1964. GUIDING INDIANS TO '54 FLAG WITH A.L. RECORD 111 WINS AND PILOTING WHITE SOX TO 1959 TITLE.

Debuting as a catcher with the Dodgers in September 1928, Al Lopez began a span of five decades wearing a major-league uniform. Although he spent all of 1929 in the minors, he won the Dodgers' starting catcher job in 1930. Lopez later represented the Dodgers in the 1934 All-Star Game and remained Brooklyn's starting catcher until being traded to the Braves after the 1935 season. Lopez was elected in 1977.

Al Lopez retired in 1947, holding the record for games caught—a record that stood for 40 years. In 1951, he began a 17-year managerial career producing American League pennants for the 1954 Cleveland Indians and the 1959 Chicago White Sox. These were the only two years between 1949 and 1964 that the Yankees did not finish in first place. Hall-of-famer Hal Newhouser said Lopez was "probably the finest manager I ever played for."

Al Lopez and Babe Ruth were participants in MLB's second All-Star Game in 1934 at New York's Polo Grounds. Many decades later, both were honored by the city of Tampa, Florida. In 1981, a plaque commemorating Ruth's 587-foot homer hit in 1919 was placed on the campus of the University of Tampa marking the spot where the ball landed after leaving Plant Field. Tampa native and hometown hero Lopez was honored in 1992 with a statue located at Al Lopez Park.

Acquired by Brooklyn in 1931, Ernie Lombardi brought with him a few prominent characteristics. A large, stocky man, he could hold seven baseballs in one enormous hand and was such a slow runner that he made other catchers look speedy; his large nose earned him the unenviable nickname "Schnozz." One of the game's finest hitting catchers, he batted over .300 ten times and, using a unique golf grip with interlocked fingers on his bat, became the first catcher to win multiple batting titles. In 1938, Lombardi caught Johnny Vander Meer's back-to-back no-hitters and won the National League's Most Valuable Player Award. Although his hall of fame career began with the Dodgers, he was traded to Cincinnati in the spring of 1932. Unfortunately for Brooklyn, his true greatness would come in another uniform. Lombardi was elected in 1986.

ERNEST NATALI LOMBARDI
BROOKLYN, N.L., 1931
CINCINNATI, N.L., 1932 - 1941
BOSTON, N.L., 1942
NEW YORK, N.L., 1943 - 1947
HIT .306 OVER 17 SEASONS DESPITE SLOWNESS AFOOT.
TEN TIMES BATTING OVER .300. WON N.L. BATTING
TITLE WITH .342 IN 1938 AND AGAIN IN 1942 WITH
.330. HELD HANDS LOW, WITH INTERLOCKING GOLF
GRIP AND QUICK STROKE. N.L. MVP IN 1938. SKILLED
RECEIVER AND HANDLER OF PITCHERS. OUTSTANDING
ARM FROM CROUCH POSITION, RIFLING THROWS
WITH SIDE-ARM RELEASE.

WAITE CHARLES HOYT
"SCHOOLBOY"

NEW YORK YANKEE PITCHER 1921-1930.
LIFETIME RECORD: 237 GAMES WON, 182
GAMES LOST, .566 AVERAGE, EARNED RUN
AVERAGE 3.59. PITCHED 5 GAMES IN 1921
WORLD SERIES AND GAVE NO EARNED RUNS.
ALSO PITCHED FOR BOSTON, DETROIT AND
PHILADELPHIA A.L. AND BROOKLYN,
NEW YORK AND PITTSBURGH N.L.

When the Dodgers signed 32-year-old pitcher Waite Hoyt early in 1932, they were adding a seven-time AL pennant winner and three-time world champion. Spending most of the 1920s with the Yankees, he won 19 or more games four times. He joined a Dodgers team that had six future hall of famers in uniform: Dazzy Vance, Al Lopez, George Kelly, Hack Wilson, manager Max Carey, and coach Casey Stengel. Hoyt spent only two months with Brooklyn, making eight appearances before moving on to the New York Giants. Five years later in 1937, he came back to the Dodgers from Pittsburgh. Working primarily as a starter, Hoyt won the final seven games of his career in a Dodger uniform, finishing with 237 wins. He pitched six games for Brooklyn in 1938 before retiring in May. Hoyt was elected in 1969.

FROM BROOKLYN GRAYS TO DODGER BLUE

Entering the major leagues in 1915 as one of the tallest players in the league, the six-foot, four-inch George Kelly earned the nickname "High Pockets." His fame began in the early 1920s with the New York Giants as a fine-hitting and outstanding fielding first baseman. Kelly led the National League in home runs in 1921 and had over 100 runs batted in each season from 1921 to 1924. In 1924, he became the first player ever to hit home runs in six consecutive games. Defensively he led all first basemen in his league in putouts and assists from 1920 to 1922. His 1,759 putouts made at first base in 1920 remains a National League record. He joined the Dodgers in 1932 and batted .317 in 64 games before retiring at the end of the season. Kelly was elected in 1973.

LEWIS ROBERT WILSON
"HACK"
NEW YORK N.L., CHICAGO N.L.,
BROOKLYN N.L., PHILADELPHIA N.L.,
1923 - 1934
ESTABLISHED MAJOR LEAGUE RECORD OF 190
RUNS BATTED IN AND NATIONAL LEAGUE HIGH
OF 56 HOMERS IN 1930. LED OR TIED FOR N.L.
HOMER TITLE FOUR TIMES. COMPILED LIFETIME
.307 BATTING AVERAGE AND DROVE IN 100 OR
MORE RUNS SIX YEARS. HIT TWO HOMERS IN
INNING IN 1925 AND THREE IN GAME IN 1930.

Teammate Clyde Sukeforth said that Hack Wilson "didn't look much like a ballplayer. He was stocky and muscular. Looked like a fireplug. Very strong." The five-foot, six-inch, 190-pound "fireplug" had one of the greatest seasons in baseball history with the 1930 Cubs. Wilson batted .356, slugged 56 home runs, and drove in 191 runs, still a major-league record. He was elected in 1979.

Hack's 56 home runs in 1930 stood as the NL record until 1998, and his 191 RBI remain one of baseball's most enduring records. Only hall-of-famers Lou Gehrig (185) and Hank Greenberg (184) came close, and there have been no serious challenges in the last 75 years. His Brooklyn highlight came in 1933; a ninth-inning, game-winning, pinch-hit inside-the-park grand slam home run at Ebbets Field—the first in Dodger history.

DEM HALL OF FAME BUMS

The first mention of "dem bums" in a New York sports page occurred in April 1937 when boxing trainer Mushky Jackson referenced fighters Jack Torrance and Abraham Simon as "dem bums." A colloquial Brooklyn expression, "dem bums" was a generic term used by locals to describe any and all whom they viewed in that light. New York taxi drivers used it referencing anyone from symphony performers to fighters to local sports teams who were not performing particularly well. That was until one summer afternoon, some say it was 1937, others 1938. *New York World-Telegram* sports cartoonist Willard Mullin hailed a cab after leaving Ebbets Field. He hopped in the back seat, and the cabbie asked, "How'd 'dem bums' do today?" Well, "dem bums" lost another one, which was, for the most part, the way things had gone for the Dodgers for the better part of two decades. In fact, Mullin had taken to referring to the Brooklynites as clowns. He had even gone so far as to create a clown character to describe the team, modeled after Emmett Kelly, the era's most famous circus clown. And in the back seat of that Brooklyn cab, the Dodger "Bum" was born.

The team was wearing the "Bums" mantle well in both 1937 and 1938 and had been doing so for some time. Since their World Series appearance in 1920, the players had virtually taken up residence in the NL's second division. They made a run at the 1924 pennant but lost it in the last four games. They placed third in 1932, fourth in 1930 and 1934, and spent 14 years bouncing between fifth, sixth, and seventh place. In 1939, Leo Durocher became the Dodgers player/manager, and immediately, the franchise turned around. They were no longer clowns yet they would manage to maintain their moniker of "Dem Bums." Born of their ineptitude on the playing field, the Dodger Bum became more popular as the team improved. In 1940, Pee Wee Reese arrived, and by mid-season, Durocher replaced himself at short with the rookie shortstop from Kentucky; in 1941, the Dodgers won their first pennant in 21 years.

Taking on the Yankees in the 1941 series, the Dodgers were down two games to one going into game four at Ebbets Field. Leading 4-3 with two outs in the ninth inning, a passed ball on strike three, which would have ended the game and tied the series, instead opened the floodgates to a 7-4 loss. "Only Dem Bums Could Have Lost World Series Game As They Did," screamed a UPI (United Press International) headline, and the Yankees eliminated "Dem Bums" the next day. The 1942 season brought more heartache. In first place since the sixth game of the season and 10 games up on August 6, "Dem Bums" managed to lose the pennant on the season's last day, despite winning their last eight games in a row.

The era that gave birth to "Dem Bums" saw an executive, two managers, and a shortstop all embark upon the baseball journeys that would land them in the hall of fame. Another nine players would pass through Flatbush, wrapping up careers that were destined for immortality. And the game's brightest star arrived for his last professional days in a big-league uniform—in the first base coaching box at Ebbets Field.

50¢

Fifth
Printing

Emmett Kelly became a frequent visitor to Ebbets Field. Carl Erskine films him while Rod Miller (No. 50) and the bat boy (center) look on. Kelly modeled this "Sad Sack" fellow after the hobos who rode the railroad boxcars during the Great Depression of the 1930s. The Dodger Bum became the symbol of anguish and frustration for the Dodger franchise of the 1940s and 1950s. In the decade spanning 1946-1956, they lost a playoff to the Cardinals in 1946 and the World Series in 1947, 1949, 1952, 1953, and 1956, all to the Yankees. And in 1951, they lost a playoff to the Giants on "the shot heard round the world." The Dodger Bum graced the cover of the Brooklyn Dodger yearbook every year from 1951 through 1957, and he invented the phrase "Wait till Next Year."

Casey Stengel began his managerial career as a player/manager with minor-league Worcester of the Eastern League in 1925. The next season, the Giants wanted him to manage their top farm team in Toledo, but Stengel was still contractually obligated to Worcester, also serving as team president. In typically comical Stengel fashion, he released himself as a player, fired himself as manager, and then resigned as president, leaving him free to join Toledo. Stengel managed there through 1931, then joined new Dodgers' manager Max Carey as first base coach for two seasons. When Carey was let go after the 1933 season, Stengel took over. In his three seasons at the Brooklyn helm, inferior talent on the field never allowed him to finish higher than fifth place. He left after 1936 to take over the Boston Braves and later had great success as manager of the Yankees.

FREDERICK CHARLES LINDSTROM
NEW YORK N.L., PITTSBURGH N.L.,
CHICAGO N.L., BROOKLYN N.L.,
1924 - 1936
COMPILED LIFETIME .311 BATTING MARK.
INCLUDING SEVEN SEASONS OF .300 OR
BETTER. ONE OF ONLY THREE PLAYERS TO
AMASS 230 OR MORE HITS A YEAR TWICE.
AS YOUNGEST PLAYER (AGE 18) IN WORLD
SERIES HISTORY, HE TIED RECORD WITH
FOUR HITS IN GAME IN 1924. EQUALLED
MAJOR LEAGUE RECORD BY COLLECTING
NINE HITS IN 1928 DOUBLEHEADER.

Third baseman Freddie Lindstrom made his major-league debut with the New York Giants in 1924, just months after his 18th birthday. Six months later, he became the youngest player to ever appear in a World Series, a distinction he still holds. Lindstrom started all seven games versus Washington; batted .333; and in game five, the rookie had four hits against the great Walter Johnson. He was elected in 1976.

Soon considered among the top-third basemen in the game, Freddie Lindstrom was named by the *Sporting News* as their major-league All-Star third sacker in 1928 and 1930. Also, in 1928, Lindstrom achieved a still-standing National League record with nine hits in a doubleheader. Lindstrom signed with Brooklyn for 1936 and had a nine-game hitting streak in May. An outfield collision on May 15 prompted his early retirement at age 30.

In 1937, seeking to add offensive production to their lineup, the Dodgers signed longtime American League batting star Heinie Manush. The left fielder had been one of the circuit's better batsmen for a decade, winning the 1926 batting title and batting over .300 in 10 different seasons. He arrived at Ebbets Field with a .333 career average. Although the 35-year-old Manush's performance had been in decline, he rebounded in 1937, hitting .333 and receiving MVP consideration. Showing flashes of his greatness, he had two hitting streaks, one of 17 games and one of 12, during the 1937 campaign. He played briefly with Brooklyn in 1938 before being released on May 15. Manush was elected in 1964.

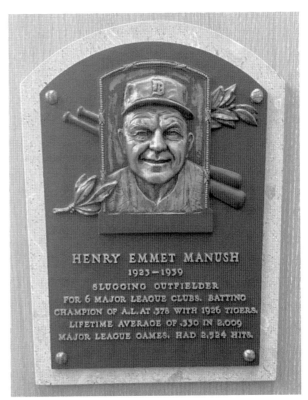

HENRY EMMET MANUSH
1923—1939
SLUGGING OUTFIELDER
FOR 6 MAJOR LEAGUE CLUBS. BATTING
CHAMPION OF A.L. AT .378 WITH 1926 TIGERS.
LIFETIME AVERAGE OF .330 IN 2,009
MAJOR LEAGUE GAMES. HAD 2,524 HITS.

LELAND STANFORD MACPHAIL
"LARRY"

DYNAMIC INNOVATIVE EXECUTIVE MADE HIS
MARK AS PROGRESSIVE HEAD OF THREE CLUBS—
CINCINNATI REDS, BROOKLYN DODGERS AND
NEW YORK YANKEES—FROM 1933 TO 1947 WON
CHAMPIONSHIPS IN BOTH LEAGUES—WITH
DODGERS IN 1941 AND YANKEES IN 1947.
PIONEERED NIGHT BALL AT CINCINNATI IN
1935, ALSO INSTALLED LIGHTS AT EBBETS FIELD
AND YANKEE STADIUM ORIGINATED PLANE
TRAVEL BY PLAYING PERSONNEL AND IDEA
OF STADIUM CLUB. HELPED SET UP EMPLOYEE
AND PLAYER PENSION PLANS.

Pioneering, innovative executive vice president and general manager Larry MacPhail (below, left) came to the Dodgers from Cincinnati in 1938. His bold moves had rescued the Reds' franchise from the brink of bankruptcy and helped create a roster that would win two National League pennants shortly after he left. The Dodgers hoped MacPhail would have a similar impact on their team, and he did not disappoint. He began renovating Ebbets Field, acquired several key players, introduced night baseball, and helped create a dramatic increase in attendance. Elevated to team president in 1939, MacPhail hired hall of fame manager Leo Durocher (below, right) to lead the team on the field. In 1942, the 52-year-old executive left the team and enlisted in the Army during World War II. He was replaced by Branch Rickey (below, center), the ultimate trailblazer. MacPhail was elected in 1978.

Slick-fielding shortstop Leo Durocher played with the Yankees, Reds, and Cardinals before being traded to the Dodgers in October 1937. He earned his nickname "Leo the Lip" because of his incessant and oftentimes critical verbalizations directed toward opponents, umpires, teammates, and managers alike. Friction had developed between Durocher and longtime Cardinals' player/manager Frankie Frisch, leading to Durocher's trade to Brooklyn. He joined a team managed by Burleigh Grimes, and though Durocher made the All-Star team, the Dodgers compiled their sixth-straight losing season. Consequently, new team executive Larry MacPhail elevated his shortstop to the manager's position, and Brooklyn was on the verge of renewed success. This began a managerial career that stretched across five decades and four franchises. He was elected in 1994.

LEO ERNEST DUROCHER
"THE LIP"
BROOKLYN, N.L., 1939-1946, 1948
NEW YORK, N.L., 1948-1955
CHICAGO, N.L., 1966-1972
HOUSTON, N.L., 1972-1973
COLORFUL, CONTROVERSIAL MANAGER FOR 24 SEASONS, WINNING 2,008 GAMES, 7TH ON ALL-TIME LIST. COMBATIVE, SWASHBUCKLING STYLE A CARRY-OVER FROM 17 YEARS AS STRONG FIELDING SHORTSTOP FOR MURDERERS ROW YANKS, GASHOUSE GANG CARDS, REDS AND DODGERS. MANAGED CLUBS TO PENNANTS IN 1941 AND 1951 AND TO WORLD SERIES WIN IN 1954. 3-TIME SPORTING NEWS MANAGER OF THE YEAR.

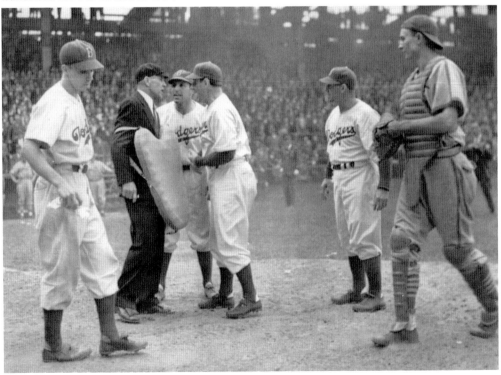

Babe Ruth sits between manager Burleigh Grimes (left) and shortstop Leo Durocher (right). Babe joined the Dodgers in June 1938, signing a $15,000 contract with Larry MacPhail, who teased Babe with the possibility of managing when Grimes left. Unbeknownst to Babe, MacPhail had already promised the job to Durocher. There was no love lost between Babe and Durocher, and some fisticuffs ensued between the pair toward the season's end. When MacPhail named Durocher the manager in October, the Babe was gone and so were his chances of managing a big-league club. However, the magnitude of his persona was once again on display. Veteran star outfielder Kiki Cuyler sat in a corner of the dugout watching him and said, "That guy is amazing. He even does something to me." Grimes said, "When he spoke, everyone listened, all but Durocher."

During the 1920s and 1930s, Kiki Cuyler was one of the finest all-around outfielders in the National League. A great line-drive hitter who routinely hit well over .300, he possessed a strong throwing arm and was a speedy base runner. A very popular player, Cuyler emerged in 1925 hitting .357 with 18 homers and 102 RBI and finishing second in MVP voting to Rogers Hornsby's Triple Crown. He was elected in 1968.

In game seven of the 1925 World Series facing Walter Johnson, Cuyler doubled in the eighth inning, driving in two runs to secure the series victory for the Pirates. He joined Brooklyn for his final major-league season in 1938 and played 68 games split between three outfield positions. Cuyler retired in mid-September with a .321 career batting average and stayed with Brooklyn as a coach for the remainder of the season.

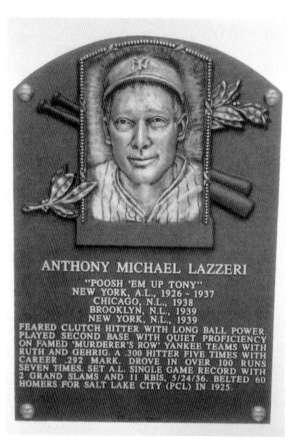

ANTHONY MICHAEL LAZZERI

"POOSH 'EM UP TONY"
NEW YORK, A.L., 1926 - 1937
CHICAGO, N.L., 1938
BROOKLYN, N.L., 1939
NEW YORK, N.L., 1939
FEARED CLUTCH HITTER WITH LONG BALL POWER.
PLAYED SECOND BASE WITH QUIET PROFICIENCY
ON FAMED 'MURDERER'S ROW' YANKEE TEAMS WITH
RUTH AND GEHRIG. A .300 HITTER FIVE TIMES WITH
CAREER .292 MARK. DROVE IN OVER 100 RUNS
SEVEN TIMES. SET A.L. SINGLE GAME RECORD WITH
2 GRAND SLAMS AND 11 RBIS, 5/24/36. BELTED 60
HOMERS FOR SALT LAKE CITY (PCL) IN 1925.

After spending most of his career with the crosstown Yankees, star second baseman and "Murderers' Row" member Tony Lazzeri came to Ebbets Field in his final season to grab a "cup of coffee." Respected for his intelligence on the field, Yankee manager Miller Huggins regarded him as the captain of his infield. Lazzeri was part of six pennants and five world championships. On May 24, 1936, he slugged three home runs and a triple and finished the game with 11 runs batted in, an American League record that still stands. Two of those home runs were grand slams and marked the first time in major-league history the feat was accomplished. Three years later, he recaptured a moment of glory with the Dodgers when Leo Durocher called on him to pinch-hit, and the always-clutch Lazzeri responded with a home run. Lazzeri was elected in 1991.

DEM HALL OF FAME BUMS

Born in Louisville, Kentucky, in 1918, Harold "Pee Wee" Reese was the Louisville Colonels' starting shortstop when Tom Yawkey's Boston Red Sox purchased that team in 1938. Reese was seen as the heir apparent to manager/shortstop Joe Cronin. With an adamant Cronin not ready to relinquish any playing time to "the sensational 19-year-old shortstop," Boston opted to sell Reese to Larry MacPhail and the Dodgers in July 1939. Nicknamed "Pee Wee" after winning a "Pee Wee" marbles tournament as a preteen, he attended his first Brooklyn training camp in 1940. Manager/shortstop Leo Durocher was impressed enough to limit his own playing time to make way for Reese. Reese was the only Dodger player from the early 1940s still with them when they moved to Los Angeles in 1958. His No. 1 was retired by the Dodgers in 1984, the same year he was elected to the hall of fame.

HAROLD HENRY "PEE WEE" REESE
BROOKLYN N.L. 1940-1957
LOS ANGELES N.L. 1958
SHORTSTOP AND CAPTAIN OF GREAT DODGER TEAMS OF 1940's AND 50's. INTANGIBLE QUALITIES OF SUBTLE LEADERSHIP ON AND OFF FIELD, COMPETITIVE FIRE AND PROFESSIONAL PRIDE COMPLEMENTED DEPENDABLE GLOVE, RELIABLE BASE-RUNNING AND CLUTCH-HITTING AS SIGNIFICANT FACTORS IN 7 DODGER PENNANTS. INSTRUMENTAL IN EASING ACCEPTANCE OF JACKIE ROBINSON AS BASEBALL'S FIRST BLACK PERFORMER.

Durocher took a liking to young Pee Wee Reese and served as a mentor early in the shortstop's career. The manager inserted Reese as Brooklyn's starter two months before his 22nd birthday. Reese later admitted that while Durocher could be tough on him at times, he was responsible for his development as a major-league shortstop. Both men were key components to the Dodgers' 100-win pennant season of 1941.

Speaking at Pee Wee Reese's funeral in 1999, teammate Joe Black recalled Reese's influence on the Dodgers and the country: "When I finally got up to Brooklyn, I went to Pee Wee and said, 'Black people love you. When you touched Jackie, you touched all of us.' With Pee Wee, it was number one on his uniform and number one in our hearts." Less than a year later, a statue of Reese was unveiled outside Louisville Slugger Park.

DEM HALL OF FAME BUMS

Twenty-year-old Joe Medwick, affectionately known as "Ducky" due to his distinctive walking style, made his major-league debut with the Cardinals in 1932 and became a perennial All-Star. Playing with the "Gashouse Gang" Cardinals in 1934, he hit .379 in their World Series victory over Detroit. Commissioner Judge Landis removed Medwick from game seven of that World Series for his own safety. After an altercation with Tiger third baseman Marvin Owen, the left fielder was pelted by apples, oranges, grapefruits, and empty bottles. In 1937, Ducky became the first player to ever have four hits in an All-Star Game and won the Triple Crown and MVP awards. Constant salary disputes prompted the Cardinals to trade the star to the Dodgers in June 1940. Medwick compiled more hits than any other Dodger from 1940 through 1942, and he was twice an All-Star. A career .336 hitter, he was elected in 1975.

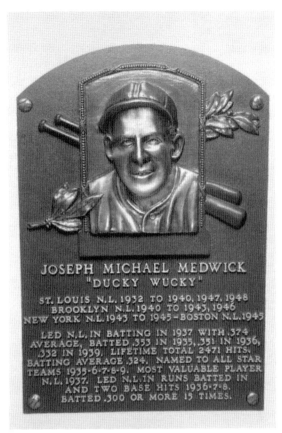

Days after Ducky Medwick's trade, the Cardinals were in Brooklyn. A verbal exchange took place in an elevator between Leo Durocher, Medwick, and Cardinals pitcher Bob Bowman. Bowman allegedly said he would "dust 'em" and "take care of both of them." Bowman's first pitch beaned Medwick, knocking him out. Larry MacPhail charged that Bowman "came to the park with the pre-meditated notion of committing murder." An investigation by the Brooklyn district attorney found intent could not be determined.

Dodgers' general manager Larry MacPhail acquired Billy Herman, the league's best second baseman, from the Cubs in 1941, believing he would bring leadership to the infield and mentorship to young shortstop Pee Wee Reese. Herman's 466 putouts in 1933 remain a league record. In 1935, his 57 doubles set a National League record for second basemen. He was elected in 1975.

DEM HALL OF FAME BUMS

Billy Herman's trade to Brooklyn paid immediate dividends, as they won 100 games and their first pennant since 1920. The Brooklyn Dodgers' infield, from left to right, first baseman Dolph Camilli, second baseman Billy Herman, shortstop Pee Wee Reese, and third baseman Arky Vaughan, pose outside Tropical Stadium in Havana during spring training in 1942. In 1943, *Baseball Magazine* featured the 10-time All-Star on the cover of its December issue.

Manager Leo Durocher (right) welcomes Billy Herman (left) after he was acquired from the Chicago Cubs for two players and $65,000 in cash. The pair competed in the National League for a decade, and Durocher was well aware of the value Herman possessed both at bat and with his glove. Herman managed in four seasons with the Pirates (1947) and the Red Sox (1964–1966) with very little success.

JOSEPH FLOYD VAUGHAN
"ARKY"
PITTSBURGH N.L. 1932-1941
BROOKLYN N.L. 1942-1948
AMONG HALL OF FAME SHORTSTOPS, HIS .318
LIFETIME BATTING AVERAGE IS SECOND ONLY TO
HONUS WAGNER'S .329. LED LEAGUE WITH .385 IN
1935. HOMERED TWICE IN 1941 ALL-STAR GAME.
FANNED ONLY 276 TIMES IN 6622 CAREER AT-BATS.
POLISHED FIELDER AND ACCOMPLISHED BASE
RUNNER, LEADING N.L. WITH 20 STOLEN BASES IN
1943.

In December 1941, the Dodgers acquired superstar shortstop Joseph Floyd "Arky" Vaughan from Pittsburgh. Vaughan was an All-Star from 1934 through 1941. A rookie in 1932, he was undeniably the premier shortstop of the decade and, by 2000, was widely recognized as a top-five shortstop of all time. He played with the Dodgers in 1942 and 1943, retired, and came back for the 1947 and 1948 seasons. One of baseball's most highly respected players, Arky tragically drowned while trying to save his friend Bill Weimer when their fishing boat capsized in 1952. Teammate "Cookie" Lavagetto said, "I never met a finer fellow or a better team man." Robert Moses summed it up best in Vaughan's SABR bio: "Overlooked and underappreciated, Vaughan ranks among the top shortstops and offensive stars of his or any era." He was elected in 1985.

DEM HALL OF FAME BUMS

When Dodgers' general manager Larry MacPhail was looking for a quality hitting outfielder for the 1941 season, another longtime Pittsburgh star became available. Signing on January 31, Paul Waner brought with him a lifetime batting average of .340, three batting titles, and the 1927 Most Valuable Player award. In his 15 years with Pittsburgh, Paul Waner, nicknamed "Big Poison," had more hits (2,868), doubles (558), and triples (187) than any other player. After only 11 games in 1941, he was released and picked up by the Boston Braves. Waner returned to Brooklyn two years later, re-signing in January 1943. At this stage of his career, he was mostly a role player, and he delivered, hitting .311 in 225 at-bats. This marked the 14th and final season he batted over .300 in his career. Big Poison was elected in 1952.

LLOYD JAMES WANER
"LITTLE POISON"
PITTSBURGH N.L., BOSTON N.L.,
CINCINNATI N.L., PHILADELPHIA N.L.,
BROOKLYN N.L. 1927-1945
MADE 223 HITS IN 1927 FIRST YEAR
WITH PITTSBURGH INCLUDING 198 SINGLES,
A MODERN MAJOR LEAGUE RECORD.
LED N.L. IN MOST SINGLES 1927-1928-1929-1931.
LIFE TOTAL 2459 HITS. BATTING AVERAGE .316.
WITH BROTHER PAUL,"BIG POISON"
STARRED IN PITTSBURGH OUTFIELD
1927-1940

Playing 14 seasons in the enormous shadow cast by his teammate and older brother Paul in Pittsburgh, Lloyd Waner's star nonetheless shined bright. An outstanding leadoff hitter, Lloyd Waner, nicknamed "Little Poison," had 223 hits, led the league in runs scored, and received MVP consideration in his rookie season. He hit .300 or better in 10 of his first 12 years in the majors. He was elected in 1967.

The ultimate contact hitter, Lloyd Waner only struck out 173 times in 18 major-league seasons. He was acquired by the Dodgers via a trade with Philadelphia in March 1943. At the time, he was working for an aircraft manufacturer supporting the war effort and did not want to leave. Lloyd eventually joined Brooklyn in the spring of 1944, served mainly as a pinch-hitter, and appeared in 15 games with his brother Paul.

THE VISIONARY

At the time of Branch Rickey's death, *New York Post* columnist Dick Young wrote, "If there was one compelling truth in Branch Rickey, while he lived—one wonderful, sincere, genuine feeling—it was his belief in human rights and a burning desire to do something about them."

Born on the banks of the Ohio River, Rickey had a passion for reading, was self-educated, and as a teen, landed a job teaching grade school to earn enough money to go to college. The middle child of three boys, he was raised in a strict, pious Methodist household in which each night, his dad would end his dinner prayer with the words, "The Lord is the head of this house." His faith was a driving force for the entirety of his life. Dodger pitcher Carl Erskine recalled guidance he received from Rickey on matters of faith. "Faith is like a red thread," Rickey told his pitcher, "that runs through every part of people's lives . . . a ball player, a truck driver, a housewife . . . it makes no difference." Rickey relied heavily on that "red thread," and it would define, motivate, and mark his path.

Speaking at a fundraising dinner for the NAACP in 1957, he urged all civil rights advocates "not to run from the word prejudice but . . . to face it and conquer it." Rickey was fully aware of the ingrained prejudice and bigotry Jackie Robinson would face. The depth and magnitude of it played out in an incident with Clay Hopper, Robinson's manager, in Montreal in 1946. In his 2007 biography *Branch Rickey, Baseball's Ferocious Gentleman*, Lee Lowenfish unveiled the tale: "All of a sudden Robinson made an incredible play on a grounder into the first base hole. 'Have you ever seen a human being make a play like that?' Rickey exclaimed." Hopper "turned away from his boss . . . and then asked quietly, 'Mr. Rickey, do you really think that a nigra is a human being?'" Sickened, he remained undeterred, and Rickey and Robinson moved forward and "conquered."

The red thread of faith brought together Branch Rickey and Jackie Robinson and would extend far beyond the baseball diamond, intermingling with the energy of two of the most powerful forces of the 20th century.

Branch Rickey's hero was Abraham Lincoln, and he hung his portrait in his office. New York sportswriter Tom Meany tabbed Rickey the "Mahatma" after he read a piece describing India's Mohandas "Mahatma" Gandhi as a combination of "your father and Tammany Hall." Mahatma means "great soul." Gandhi was a hero of Dr. Martin Luther King, who applied Gandhi's concepts of "non-violent passive resistance and civil disobedience" to the American civil rights movement. King hung a portrait of Gandhi in the dining room of his home. On August 28, 1945, Jackie Robinson met in Rickey's office where Mahatma unveiled his "noble experiment." It was in this meeting that Rickey told Jackie, "I'm looking for someone who has the courage not to fight back." On August 28, 1963, eighteen years from that very day, Jackie and Rachel Robinson, with their son David, partook in the March on Washington where, standing before the monument to Branch Rickey's hero, Martin Luther King delivered his iconic "I Have a Dream" speech. Wesley Branch Rickey himself was the red thread of faith running through people's lives.

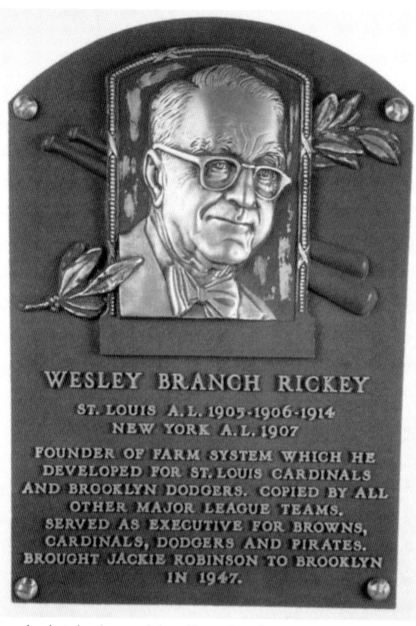

WESLEY BRANCH RICKEY
ST. LOUIS A.L. 1905-1906-1914
NEW YORK A.L. 1907
FOUNDER OF FARM SYSTEM WHICH HE
DEVELOPED FOR ST. LOUIS CARDINALS
AND BROOKLYN DODGERS. COPIED BY ALL
OTHER MAJOR LEAGUE TEAMS.
SERVED AS EXECUTIVE FOR BROWNS,
CARDINALS, DODGERS AND PIRATES.
BROUGHT JACKIE ROBINSON TO BROOKLYN
IN 1947.

In the past decade it has become fashionable to downplay, disregard, or even vanquish the accomplishments of past American generations. In 2014, sportscaster Len Berman questioned Rachel Robinson regarding Rickey's motives in signing Jack, hinting it was a financial ploy to sell tickets. He was "a seriously committed person," she replied. "He wanted to see change take place and he wanted to be a part of that . . . It had to do with changing society." In a 2010 interview for the Visionary Project, she spoke of Jackie and Mr. Rickey. Rickey "was very devoted to his family, very devoted to his religion," she said. "They clicked mostly around their commitment to family, to religion. It made him easy to talk to about really difficult things." Jack Robinson and Mr. Rickey became very devoted to each other. Rickey was elected in 1967.

THE VISIONARY

Coaching at Ohio Wesleyan, Branch Rickey first encountered segregation in baseball. He often told the tale of his catcher Charles Thomas, a Black man who often roomed with Coach Rickey. Thomas was sitting on his cot one night, lamenting his skin color and wishing he could "turn it white." Thomas became a dentist, Rickey became a civil rights activist, and the two remained friends their entire lives.

In 1920, Branch Rickey became the vice president and manager of the St. Louis Cardinals. By the time he left in 1942, the Cardinals had constructed the first ballpark exclusively for a team's spring training in Bradenton, Florida; invented the minor-league system; designed the Cardinal logo; and won six NL pennants and four World Series. Their farm system produced hall-of-famers Dizzy Dean, Joe Medwick, Enos Slaughter, and Stan Musial.

Clay Hopper stands with Branch Rickey behind Jackie Robinson in Daytona Beach in 1946. Hopper had been working for Rickey for nearly two decades, and despite his ingrained prejudice and fear of reprisals from his friends and neighbors in Mississippi, he pledged to Rickey that he would treat Robinson like "any other player." Rickey bluntly gave him "no other choice." Hopper and Robinson both delivered; Jackie hit .349, leading Hopper's Royals to an International League title.

The Mahatma and his grandson keep watchful eyes over their newly constructed spring facility in Vero Beach. Batting cages, pitching machines, and batting helmets, which were making headway in other places, were ubiquitous in Dodgertown. Yet another example of Rickey's superlative vision is that, in 1948, he determined that OBP was more important than batting average in evaluating a player's value. It would take the MLB six decades to catch up to that fact.

THE VISIONARY

Ever the innovator, in the spring of 1950, Branch Rickey (left) collaborated with General Electric to test an "electronic" umpire. Pee Wee Reese stands in while manager Barney Shotton (kneeling and pointing), R.F. Shea (from GE), Jackie Robinson, Duke Snider, and umpire Bill Stewart (checkered shirt) look on. Rickey wanted to create a device that would assist pitchers working on pitch location.

Walter O'Malley purchased Branch Rickey's share of the Dodgers in the fall of 1950, and within days, Rickey became the vice president and general manager of the Pirates, who were abysmal. They remained terrible throughout Rickey's tenure, which ended in 1955. However, during that time, Rickey "stole" Roberto Clemente from the Dodgers in the Rule 5 draft and acquired Dick Groat, Bill Mazeroski, Elroy Face, and Vern Law, all key components of the Pirates' 1960 world championship team.

Jackie Robinson was effusive in his praise, admiration, and love for the man he called "Mr. Rickey." He never missed an opportunity to sing his praises, referring to him in his own hall of fame induction speech as mentor, advisor, friend, and—the ultimate praise—"the man I consider a father." In his 1972 autobiography, he wrote of Rickey, "As I mourned for him, I realized how much our relationship deepened after I left baseball. . . . Branch Rickey treated me like a son. . . . At Mr. Rickey's funeral, I was deeply disturbed at the lack of recognition paid to him. . . . A couple of Black players were there." Robinson felt they owed him for creating "the opportunity . . . to play. . . . I could not understand why some of the Black superstars, who earn so much money in the game today, had not even sent flowers or telegrams."

THE VISIONARY

BASEBALL IN

BLACK AND WHITE

Jackie Robinson was a track star; a football star; the only four-sport letterman in the history of the University of California, Los Angeles (UCLA); a Kansas City Monarch for a year; a Los Angeles Red Devil for another; and for 10 years, he wore No. 42 for the Brooklyn Dodgers. In those 10 years, his performance on the field placed him in the true elite of the game; one of the most dominant, most valuable, most productive players to ever wear a uniform. It all pales when measured against what he overcame, what he endured, and what he did for his family, his race, his team, baseball, America, and the world.

A microcosm of the totality of his challenge played out in the fifth game of his rookie season. The Phillies were in town, and they were managed by Ben Chapman, who was raised in Birmingham, Alabama. Known as a premier bench jockey, the manager took his "art" to a new level that April afternoon in Brooklyn. Twenty-five years later, Robinson recalled, "Philly was the worst, Ben Chapman was quite vicious. He was not only vicious as far as Black people were concerned, I think he was anti-everything." Chapman readily admitted he had instructed his players to "give it to Robinson without restraint. . . . Call Robinson anything and everything they wanted," assuring them they had his "unswerving support." He spewed his cacophony of cruelty ranging from the banality of things, such as "Hey nigger, come over here and shine my shoes" and "Why ain't you out pick'n cotton?," to draconian comments regarding Robinson infecting the wives of his teammates with sexually transmitted diseases.

Robinson answered the hatred with aplomb, grace, and dignity, never letting on to what he revealed in his 1972 autobiography about that day: It "brought me nearer to cracking up than I ever had been." Against insurmountable odds, withstanding unimaginable pressure and cruelty, Jackie Robinson endured. In calling upon the very best of himself to withstand the worst of America, he offered his countrymen a choice to either succumb to hate or summon the very best of themselves.

What Jackie Robinson accomplished on the field was truly remarkable, but what he accomplished off the field was truly transformative. In a 2016 interview, Rachel Robinson spoke of Jackie's driving force both on and off the field: He had "a passionate belief in equality for all people and he was determined to advance that cause." He followed his passion, and with dignity and strength, he spoke openly and frankly on matters of race and equality. The Reverend Dr. Martin Luther King Jr. recognized the force that was Jack Roosevelt Robinson. Appearing on Larry King's show, Dr. King was introduced as "the founder of the civil rights movement," to which Dr. King replied, "Jackie Robinson was the founder of the civil rights movement."

Jesse Jackson delivered Jackie Robinson's eulogy, calling him "a rock in the water creating concentric circles and ripples of new possibilities. He was medicine . . . immunized by God from catching the diseases that he fought. . . . He had the capacity to wear glory with grace. Jackie's body was a temple of God, an instrument of peace."

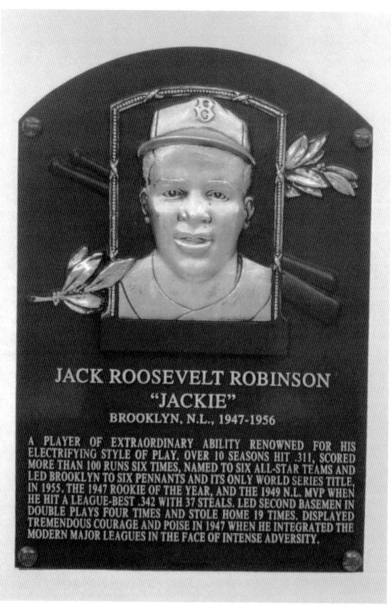

JACK ROOSEVELT ROBINSON
"JACKIE"
BROOKLYN, N.L., 1947-1956

A PLAYER OF EXTRAORDINARY ABILITY RENOWNED FOR HIS ELECTRIFYING STYLE OF PLAY. OVER 10 SEASONS HIT .311, SCORED MORE THAN 100 RUNS SIX TIMES, NAMED TO SIX ALL-STAR TEAMS AND LED BROOKLYN TO SIX PENNANTS AND ITS ONLY WORLD SERIES TITLE, IN 1955. THE 1947 ROOKIE OF THE YEAR, AND THE 1949 N.L. MVP WHEN HE HIT A LEAGUE-BEST .342 WITH 37 STEALS. LED SECOND BASEMEN IN DOUBLE PLAYS FOUR TIMES AND STOLE HOME 19 TIMES. DISPLAYED TREMENDOUS COURAGE AND POISE IN 1947 WHEN HE INTEGRATED THE MODERN MAJOR LEAGUES IN THE FACE OF INTENSE ADVERSITY.

A breakdown of modern metrics reveals Jackie Robinson's greatness on the field. There is no metric to measure the impact of his life upon humanity. At his induction, he said, " This . . . could not have happened without . . . guidance I've had from three of the most wonderful people I know. . . . My advisor, a wonderful friend, a man who I consider a father, Mr. Branch Rickey. My mother who taught me so much of the important things in life. . . . My wife . . . a wonderful inspiration to me . . . she has guided me throughout our marriage. . . . I couldn't be here today without her." On the base supporting his statue at Dodger Stadium is engraved his simple but powerful words, "A life is not important except in the impact it has on other lives." Jackie's been gone for over a half-century yet the magnitude of his impact reverberates across the decades, and the "concentric circles . . . and ripples of new possibilities" he created live on. He was elected in 1962.

BASEBALL IN BLACK AND WHITE

Lt. Jackie Robinson, a football star at UCLA (as seen below) was drafted into the Army in the spring of 1942 and assigned to a segregated cavalry unit at Fort Riley, Kansas. It was in the Army that Robinson began to actively challenge America's Jim Crow laws. Asked to join the base's integrated football team, he refused after learning he would sit out games in which the opponents chose not to play against Blacks. A qualified candidate for Officer Candidate School, he was denied admission until Joe Louis intervened on his behalf. At Fort Hood, Texas, his clash with Jim Crow culminated with his refusal to move to the back of the bus, leading to a court-martial charge for which he was acquitted. "It was a small victory," Robinson said, "for I had learned that I was in two wars, one against the foreign enemy, the other against prejudice at home." The war against prejudice would continue throughout his life.

Jackie Robinson played for the Kansas City Monarchs in the Negro Leagues in 1945, and it was there where he continued to "send forth ripples of new possibilities." Teammate and fellow hall-of-famer Buck O'Neil related an oft-told tale to talk show host David Letterman in 1998 of a "filling station" stop, one night in Oklahoma. While the attendant was filling the gas tank of the bus, Robinson disembarked and headed inside. "Where you going, boy?" the attendant asked. "I'm going to use the restroom," came his reply. "You can't go in there," he was told. Robinson turned back to the bus and said, "Take that hose out of the tank." The players used the restroom that night and never again used a gas station that would not allow them the use of the restroom facilities. Robinson also brought the "Negro League style of play" to Brooklyn, stealing home 19 times during his career.

BASEBALL IN BLACK AND WHITE

Branch Rickey signed Jackie Robinson to a Montreal Royals contract for the 1946 season. In April 1947, the Brooklyn Dodgers purchased his contract, and the noble experiment was on. In a 2010 interview with the MLB Network, Rachel Robinson recalled that first game: "It was a cold day. . . . In Brooklyn, the fans were always on Jack's side. He got a rousing ovation. . . . When I think back on that day, I have a feeling of having survived something important. . . . We knew we were part of something in a permanent way." In a 1972 interview with talk show host Dick Cavett, Jackie said of Branch Rickey, "I would have jumped off the bridge if he told me to do it. That's how much I believed in him. He was a man who was sincere and dedicated and willing to lend that helping hand that is so needed today in terms of the problems we face."

FINAL DAILY NEWS BROOKLYN QUEENS LONG ISLAND

DODGERS PURCHASE ROBBY GIANTS WIN, RIP FELLER

DODGERS CLUB HOUSE

KEEP OUT

Jackie Robinson, first Negro to be admitted to major leagues, enters Dodger clubhouse.—Story on page 63

Pictured here on opening day in 1947 is the starting infield of the Brooklyn Dodgers, made up of, from left to right, Spider Jorgensen (third base), Pee Wee Reese (shortstop), Eddie Stanky (second base), and Jackie Robinson (first base). Initially, some of Robinson's teammates were not on board with the noble experiment, signing a petition against the idea. However, the vitriol that some opponents and fans heaped upon Robinson served as a bonding force for the team. As one pundit put it, "The players rallied to his defense, that caused a glue on the club that molded them into a pennant-winning team." In the midst of the vitriol came economic opportunities as well. The *Pittsburg Courier* reported in May 1947, "A nationally known bakery has paid Jackie a reported $500 to endorse its bread." Robinson would later endorse, among other things, hats, a baseball board game, and Chesterfield cigarettes, and he graced the front of the Wheaties box more than once.

Although April 15, 1947, has become the designated date of Jackie Robinson's integration into baseball, it actually occurred on March 17, 1946, in Daytona Beach, Florida, at a ballpark that now bears his name. There were two Black players on the Royals that day: Robinson and Johnny Wright (second from left). A historical marker reads, "Just as Branch Rickey chose Jackie Robinson, he chose Daytona Beach as the site for his 'noble experiment.'" Dr. Bethune, founder of what is now Bethune Cookman University, a 50-year driving force in the civil rights movement, created what writer Jules Tygiel called "an island of enlightenment in a sea of bigotry." Wendell Smith noted that Daytona Beach's "healthy racial atmosphere can be attributed to the excellent work done by the faithful and energetic Mary McLeod Bethune." The Robinsons stayed at the home of Black politician Joe Harris and often dined at the college. In 1954, they returned when Jackie received an honorary degree from the college and visited with Dr. Bethune.

From left to right, Gene Hermanski, Jackie Robinson, and Gil Hodges are pictured above after an April 1949 game in which they were involved in a triple play. Their fingers indicate which out each recorded. On Jackie Robinson Day 2020, Vin Scully related the tale of an ominous visit to Crosley Field, Cincinnati, in June 1950. Robinson received a death threat stating that he would be killed on the field. In an effort to break the tension in a very tense pregame locker room, Hermanski suggested the entire team wear No. 42 so the perpetrator could not tell the difference. Hermanski lived to see the entire league wearing No. 42. Gil Hodges, whom Robinson called "the core of the Brooklyn Dodgers" and Jackie Robinson (below) both succumbed to heart attacks in 1972; Hodges's heart attack happened just 12 days before opening day, while Robinson's was just two days after the World Series ended.

In the midst of the 1949 season, in which Jackie Robinson was the first Black man to win an MVP award (below), Jackie and Rachel Robinson, who was always at his side, traveled to Washington, DC, for his testimony before the House Un-American Activities Committee. The subject was the "loyalty of blacks to the United States." He said in part, "I don't pretend to be an expert on communism or any other kind of political-ism . . . but I am an expert on being a colored American." He then cautioned Americans: "Just because communists kick up a big fuss over racial discrimination when it suits their purpose . . . denounces injustice in the courts, police brutality and lynching . . . doesn't change the truth of (their) charges." He countered the charge that "communists were stirring up Negroes" by telling the committee, that "Negroes were stirred up long before there was a communist party."

In 1956, Jackie Robinson's last season, Frank Robinson was the first ever unanimous choice for NL Rookie of the Year. Jackie won the inaugural Major League Award in 1947, and in 1949, the MLB began selecting one in each league. Including Jackie, the first six NL recipients were Black. In October 1972 (below), Jackie was honored before the second game of the World Series. He spoke with gratitude and closed with "I am extremely proud and pleased to be here this afternoon, but must admit I am going to be tremendously more pleased and more proud when I look at that third base coaching line one day and see a Black face managing in baseball." Nine days later, Jackie Robinson was dead. Two years later, the Cleveland Indians named Frank Robinson baseball's first Black manager.

BASEBALL IN BLACK AND WHITE

In his 1972 autobiography, Jackie Robinson said of Martin Luther King, "He is my idol." They received honorary degrees together at Howard University in 1957. Dr. King referred to Jackie as "a pilgrim that walked in the lonesome byways toward the high road of Freedom. He was a sit-inner before sit-ins, a freedom rider before freedom rides." Robinson was in Birmingham with King in May 1963 for the Children's Campaign and with him on the steps of the Lincoln Memorial three months later. In June 1963, following the murder of Medgar Evers, Robinson wrote an impassioned plea to President Kennedy, imploring him "to utilize every federal facility to protect a man sorely needed for this era . . . to millions Martin King symbolizes the bearing forward of the torch for freedom so savagely wrested from the dying grip of Medgar Evers." Sadly, Robinson would see both Kennedy and King fall to assassins' bullets.

Jackie Robinson and Bob Feller arrived in Boston in January 1962 to be honored by the Boston chapter of the Baseball Writers' Association of America (BBWAA). Babe Ruth's widow, Claire, presented Roger Maris with an award for breaking Babe's home run record in 1961, but Robinson stole the show, receiving two standing ovations. Feller introduced Robinson, saying, "I'll be proud to walk into Cooperstown beside you." Robinson told the *Boston Globe*'s Jack Barry, "Maybe some youngsters will learn of my struggles . . . and the election will encourage them to battle the obstacles." Branch Rickey was the first one Robinson called when learning of his election to the hall of fame. Of Rachel Robinson, First Lady Michele Obama said in 2016, "She was his equal in every way, in every way." And then added "Without Rachel, you don't get Jackie Robinson"—a sentiment Jackie echoed throughout his life.

Jackie Robinson, accompanied by his son and the son of Roy Campanella, visited the Lincoln Statue outside the Essex County Courthouse in Newark, New Jersey, in 1951. Robinson could not have envisioned that the residents of New Jersey would visit his own 14-foot-tall bronze statue in Journal Square in Jersey City. Sculpted by Susan Wagner, it was commissioned by the Jackie Robinson Foundation and dedicated in 1998. (Photography by Mark Kaufman.)

Bill Russell (left) and Don Newcombe (right) lead the pallbearers carrying Jackie Robinson to his rest. Both felt Robinson's "ripples of new possibilities." Newcombe became the first Black pitcher to win 20 games, start a World Series game, win a Cy Young Award, and an MVP award. Russell won two NCAA basketball championships, 11 NBA championships, and an Olympic gold medal, and he became the first Black man to coach a major American sport team, the Boston Celtics.

Gene Hermanski's comment "We should all wear 42" on that long-ago summer day broke the tension of an intensely perilous moment. No one could ever have imagined the prophecy embedded in his words. On April 15, 1997, Jackie's No. 42 was retired by MLB. Rachel Robinson addressed the crowd at Dodger Stadium: "This anniversary gives us the opportunity to celebrate, as a nation, the triumphs of the past and the social progress which has occurred. And . . . the opportunity to reassess the challenges of the present." Frank Robinson said on the day he became manager of the Cleveland Indians, "I thank the Lord that Jackie Robinson was the man who was in that position. . . . If he wasn't, it would have set back the whole idea of signing more Black players . . . I wish . . . Jackie Robinson could be here today." Every April 15, MLB celebrates Jackie Robinson Day, and 750 players, of all colors and ethnicities, wear No. 42 in tribute to the man who sent forth those "ripples of new possibilities."

BASEBALL IN BLACK AND WHITE

THE BOYS OF SUMMER

"The Boys of Summer" is a remarkably loving and romanticized term that has grown synonymous with the Brooklyn Dodgers of the 1940s and 1950s. In 1939, Welch poet Dylan Thomas penned his poem *I See the Boys of Summer*, a tale of summers, winters, and love. In 1972, sportswriter, novelist, biographer, poet, and Dodger fan Roger Kahn penned *The Boys of Summer*, a tale of summers, winters, and love played out in the backdrop of Ebbets Field. The subtitle encompasses its scope and purpose, the classic narrative of growing up within shouting distance of Ebbets Field, covering the Jackie Robinson Dodgers, and what has happened to everybody since. It is a chronology of a time when the sports world was dominated by baseball, boxing, and horse racing, and New York was the king of the baseball world.

The Brooklyn Dodgers were an entity unlike any other in the history of baseball. "They lived in the community, blocks away from each other," said Pat Cooper in the documentary *Brooklyn Dodgers: Ghosts of Flatbush.* They took jobs in Brooklyn in the off-season. Some sold cars or insurance, and Jackie Robinson sold household appliances. They sat on the stoop together, and when Gil and Joan Hodges' first child was born, "It was as if the whole neighborhood was having a baby."

Enter Roger Kahn, a little boy led to baseball's altar by his dad, like so many of the sons of the "Greatest Generation," to pledge fealty to the Dodgers in what became, for millions, a quasi-spiritual experience. Kahn chronicled his early fandom and his days as a nascent reporter covering the 1952 and 1953 Dodgers for the defunct *New York Herald Tribune*. Two decades later, he revisited his "boys" to chronicle where life had taken them. Never paid enough to be set up for life, he found them, among other things, tending bar and installing elevators. And dealing with the bittersweet journey that life provides to all.

Five of those boys found immortality in Cooperstown. It was a rare experience that five teammates would play so long together and be ushered into Cooperstown. In the early stages of Kahn's *The Boys of Summer* book release, death claimed its first "boy" when Gil Hodges was felled by a heart attack. Before the year's end, Jackie Robinson was gone. Life dealt a cruel fate to Roy "Campy" Campanella, the gritty MVP catcher, when an auto accident sentenced him to life in a chair as a quadriplegic. He redefined himself and the word "grit." Pee Wee Reese became an octogenarian before cancer claimed him in 1999, and Duke Snider, the "Duke of Flatbush," reached the new millennium and passed away in 2011.

Roger Kahn wrote, "It is fiercely difficult for the athlete to grow old, but to age with dignity and with courage cuts close to what it is to be a man. And most of them have aged that way with dignity, with courage and with hope." In 2002, *Sports Illustrated* ranked *The Boys of Summer* the second-greatest sports book ever written. In 2006, Kahn was inducted into the National Jewish Sports Hall of Fame, and in 2015, book sales surpassed three million copies in 90 printings. Kahn joined his boys in 2020, passing at the age of 92.

The Boys of Summer remain alive in Kahn's testament to that time when baseball was the undisputed American pastime and New York reigned as baseball's undisputed king.

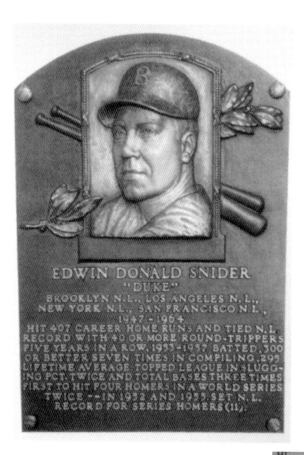

EDWIN DONALD SNIDER
"DUKE"
BROOKLYN N.L., LOS ANGELES N.L.,
NEW YORK N.L., SAN FRANCISCO N.L.,
1947-1964
HIT 407 CAREER HOME RUNS AND TIED N.L.
RECORD WITH 40 OR MORE ROUND-TRIPPERS
FIVE YEARS IN A ROW. 1953-1957 BATTED .300
OR BETTER SEVEN TIMES IN COMPILING .295
LIFETIME AVERAGE. TOPPED LEAGUE IN SLUGG-
ING PCT. TWICE AND TOTAL BASES THREE TIMES
FIRST TO HIT FOUR HOMERS IN A WORLD SERIES
TWICE -- IN 1952 AND 1955. SET N. L.
RECORD FOR SERIES HOMERS (11).

During baseball's golden age of the 1950s, all-time greats roamed center field for each of New York's three teams. For the Yankees, it was Mickey Mantle, the Giants had Willie Mays, and the Brooklyn Dodgers had Duke Snider. The trio dominated the decade, and Brooklyn's Duke of Flatbush had more home runs and runs batted in than either Mays or Mantle. He hit the last home run at Ebbets Field. Snider was elected in 1980.

A four-sport letterman at Compton High School in Los Angeles, Duke Snider signed with Brooklyn after attending a Dodger free agent tryout camp in 1943. He made his major-league debut two days after Jackie Robinson in 1947. This boy of summer returned home to his native Los Angeles for his 12th season and the Dodgers' first in Los Angeles. His 16-season Dodger career still stands as one of the most productive in franchise history.

THE BOYS OF SUMMER

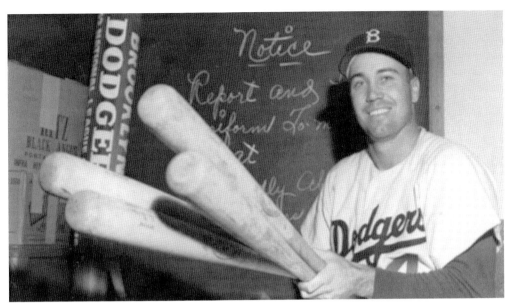

Seeing his great potential, Branch Rickey was a big supporter of the young Snider. In spring training 1949, he instructed him to watch from behind the batting cage to learn to identify the pitches. When the coaching staff was satisfied with his ability to do so, he was allowed to hit. Snider became the regular center fielder in the 1949 pennant-winning season and routinely displayed his powerful swing, graceful outfield play, and speed on the base paths.

In 1950, Duke Snider had a breakout season, leading the league in hits (199) and total bases (343) and being elected to his first of seven-straight All-Star teams. On May 30, he is celebrating with, from left to right, Robinson, Reese, and Campanella after hitting three home runs. The Brooklyn Eagles' Tommy Holmes wrote, "Each of his blasts rang out like the crack of doom and there are few who ever witnessed a more concentrated display of explosive batting power."

Twenty-four-year-old birthday boy Duke Snider celebrates with fans before a game at Ebbets Field on September 19, 1950. He thrilled his admirers that day with a gift of his own—three hits, two home runs, and five RBI to help beat the Pittsburgh Pirates 14-3. Though he developed a somewhat temperamental reputation and proneness to outbursts when things did not go well, he remained immensely popular with local fans throughout his career.

From left to right, Duke Snider, Jackie Robinson, and Pee Wee Reese carry an oversized bat representing their 1952 National League championship prior to a World Series game at Ebbets Field. Although they lost the series in seven games, Snider swung a very big bat of his own, hitting .345, slugging four home runs, and driving in eight. Snider's four home runs tied a World Series record shared by Babe Ruth and Lou Gehrig.

THE BOYS OF SUMMER

In 1943, at the age of 19, Gil Hodges played one game with the Dodgers just two weeks before enlisting in the Marine Corps. He returned to the Dodgers after serving as a gunner in the 16th Anti-Aircraft Battalion, where he received the Bronze Star at the Battle of Okinawa. Universally respected as one of baseball's most decent and honorable men, Hodges's quiet, strong leadership was essential to the Dodgers' success from 1947 through the 1950s. Arthur Daley of the *New York Times* said, "I believe Gil to have been one of the finest men I met in sports or out of it," In 2021, a half-century after he left the field, Cooperstown called for Gil Hodges. Son Gil Jr. said, "It's a great thing that happened for our family. We are all thrilled that Mom got to see it, being 95 . . . we've all waited a long time, and we are just grateful and thankful that it's finally come to fruition."

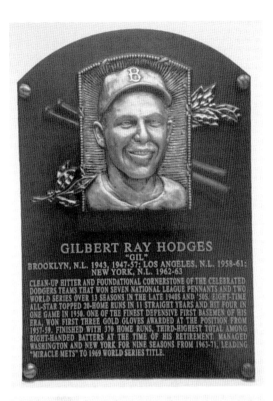

Hodges returned in 1947, catching 24 games. With the arrival of Roy Campanella in 1948, the athletic Hodges transitioned easily to first base where he became the major league's premier first baseman of his time. Through the 1950s, he led all major-league first basemen in home runs (310), runs (890), hits (1,491), RBI (1,001), and total bases (2,733). Equally adept defensively, he consistently led or was among the league leaders in putouts, assists, double plays, and fielding percentage. After the creation of the Gold Glove Award in 1957, Hodges won it for the first three years. Pee Wee Reese once claimed Hodges to be such a great defender, he could play first "bare-handed. . . . If you had a son, it would be a great thing to have him grow up to be just like Gil Hodges." Roy Campanella said simply, "Gil Hodges is a hall-of-fame man."

A natural leader, Hodges managed five years with the Washington Senators and four more with the New York Mets. In 1969, he piloted the "Amazin' Mets" from ninth place to a world championship. Tom Seaver said of him, "He was the most important person in my career . . . he taught me professionalism." In 1978, the Memorial Parkway Bridge in Brooklyn was rededicated in his name. A space was left to one day hold his hall of fame plaque—a space that now can be filled.

The Dodgers' third Black player, Roy Campanella, nicknamed "Campy," arrived in 1948. He was the second Black man to win the MVP award, the second to be enshrined in Cooperstown, and the first to win multiple (three) MVP awards. Differences aside, he held a deep abiding respect and gratitude for Jackie Robinson. "Jackie made things easy for us," he said. "[Because of him] I'm just another guy playing baseball." He was elected in 1969.

Modern metrics rank Campy as one of the top-five catchers of all time. However, there is no measuring what he became to millions of Americans following his auto accident in 1958, which rendered him a quadriplegic. He was 36 years old when that car wreck placed him in a wheelchair, in which he would live the last 36 years of his life. The initial post-accident prognosis was positive and hopeful that he could, in fact, come back. It proved not to be the case, and emerging from the darkness and despair of his situation, he, in the words of Carl Erskine, "chose life." Roy Campanella became the most famous American living his life in a wheelchair. Using his platform and ferocious competitive spirit, he became a lifelong, passionate advocate for the physically handicapped.

THE BOYS OF SUMMER

Billy Martin is thrown out at home on the losing end of a collision with Campy, ending game four of the 1953 World Series. Brooklyn won the game and evened the series at two games apiece. Martin said that running into the five-foot, nine-inch, 190-pound catcher was like "hitting the Rock of Gibraltar." The Yankees won the next two games and their fifth-straight World Series.

As often as not, these six Boys of Summer occupied the two through seven spots in Brooklyn's lineup. From left to right are (first row) Jackie Robinson, Carl Furillo, and Pee Wee Reese; (second row) Roy Campanella, Gil Hodges, and Duke Snider. Combined, they played 70 seasons in Brooklyn and made 41 All-Star teams. There were four MVPs, three stolen base champs, two batting champs, an RBI champ, and a Rookie of the Year. They collectively played in 35 World Series and, in 1955, were world champs.

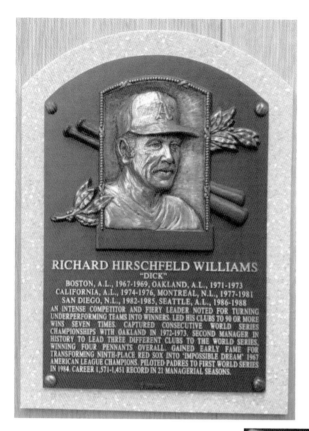

RICHARD HIRSCHFELD WILLIAMS
"DICK"
BOSTON, A.L., 1967-1969; OAKLAND, A.L., 1971-1973
CALIFORNIA, A.L., 1974-1976; MONTREAL, N.L., 1977-1981
SAN DIEGO, N.L., 1982-1985; SEATTLE, A.L., 1986-1988
AN INTENSE COMPETITOR AND FIERY LEADER NOTED FOR TURNING
UNDERPERFORMING TEAMS INTO WINNERS. LED HIS CLUBS TO 90 OR MORE
WINS SEVEN TIMES. CAPTURED CONSECUTIVE WORLD SERIES
CHAMPIONSHIPS WITH OAKLAND IN 1972-1973. SECOND MANAGER IN
HISTORY TO LEAD THREE DIFFERENT CLUBS TO THE WORLD SERIES,
WINNING FOUR PENNANTS OVERALL. GAINED EARLY FAME FOR
TRANSFORMING NINTH-PLACE RED SOX INTO 'IMPOSSIBLE DREAM' 1967
AMERICAN LEAGUE CHAMPIONS. PILOTED PADRES TO FIRST WORLD SERIES
IN 1984. CAREER 1,571-1,451 RECORD IN 21 MANAGERIAL SEASONS.

Inducted into Cooperstown as a manager, Dick Williams began his baseball career with the Brooklyn Dodgers. Signing in 1947, he began a decade-long association with the franchise. In May 1950, he appeared as an extra in *The Jackie Robinson Story*, and the following year, he made his Brooklyn debut. His 21-year managerial career garnered him four pennants and two world championships. He was elected in 2008.

Williams was always grateful to Robinson for the support he gave him in his early years. He left Brooklyn in 1956, and his journeyman career ended in Boston in 1964. Three years later, the 38-year-old rookie manager piloted the Boston Red Sox "Impossible Dream" team to the 1967 World Series. He became only the second manager to lead three different teams to the World Series.

THE BOYS OF SUMMER

GOODBYE, FLATBUSH;
HELLO, HOLLYWOOD

The 1952 season ended in heartbreak for the Dodgers as they dropped the sixth and seventh World Series games at home. The following year began a series of events that would ultimately rip the heart out of Dodger fans, Flatbush, and the entire borough of Brooklyn.

Boston Braves owner Lou Perini moved his franchise to Milwaukee in 1953. The Browns left St. Louis for Baltimore in 1954, and in 1955, the A's forsook Philadelphia for Kansas City. And as rumblings about Brooklyn were heard, Dem Bums continued to succeed on the field, taking the 1953 pennant, finishing second in 1954, and, in 1955, finally capturing the Holy Grail.

In February 1952, the sports rumor mill reported the Brooklyn Dodgers were contemplating "moving their franchise to New Orleans." With the Dodgers dominating the NL in August 1953 on their way to successive NL pennants and their fourth in seven years, Walter O'Malley responded to reports of a possible move to Los Angeles. "The invitation is not being considered," he said. Four days after Brooklyn fell in the 1953 World Series, a Calgary newspaper reported that "the idea of the Dodgers going to Montreal is being kicked around quite vigorously in baseball today." The Twin Cities of Minnesota joined in the foray of speculation of future Dodger homes, and the idea of nearby Jersey City grew traction when the Dodgers agreed to play some "home games" there in 1957. In all the tumult and folderol, there was never a doubt that O'Malley's preference was to remain in Brooklyn.

Models of the $6 million all-purpose domed facility excited the Brooklynites; however, it never got off the ground, and by opening day of 1957, it was a foregone conclusion that the Brooklyn Dodgers were bound for the West Coast.

O'Malley was painted as the villain in this heartbreaking episode, and in many circles, he remains so to this day. The vitriol held by Brooklynites are best illustrated by a joke: "If a Brooklyn man finds himself in a room with Hitler, Stalin, and O'Malley, but has only two bullets, what does he do? Shoot O'Malley twice." However, when the emotion is removed from the equation, Robert Moses emerges as a significant player in the Dodgers' departure. The simultaneous holder of the positions of chairman of the New York State Council of Parks and the commissioner of the New York Department of Parks and Recreation, he was one of the most powerful figures in state politics. Motivated by a personal animus of O'Malley and a desire for a new stadium in Flushing Meadows, he blocked every effort to purchase any land in Brooklyn's West End, which would facilitate the construction of a new stadium. O'Malley's view was simply that "we are the Brooklyn Dodgers, and if we are 30 miles away or 3,000 miles away, we are no longer the Brooklyn Dodgers."

In 1958, the Dodgers said goodbye to Flatbush and made more money than any other MLB team, enabling them to pay off their debt. They won the World Series in 1959, moved into Dodger Stadium in 1962, and won the World Series in 1963 and 1965. In 2021, the team led MLB in revenue and remain one of the most successful sports franchises in the world.

WALTER O'MALLEY
BROOKLYN, N.L., 1943-1957
LOS ANGELES, N.L., 1958-1979

AN INFLUENTIAL AND VISIONARY OWNER WHO INSPIRED BASEBALL'S MOVE WEST IN 1957. RELOCATED DODGERS FROM BROOKLYN TO LOS ANGELES AND OPENED NEW MARKETS FOR THE MAJOR LEAGUE GAME. SERVED AS PRESIDENT AND PRINCIPAL OWNER WHEN HIS CLUBS WON FOUR WORLD SERIES CHAMPIONSHIPS (1955, 1959, 1963 AND 1965) AND 11 PENNANTS. MAINTAINED AFFORDABLE TICKET PRICES WHILE GENERATING RECORD ATTENDANCE. DRIVING FORCE BEHIND DESIGN, CONSTRUCTION AND FINANCING OF DODGER STADIUM, A BENCHMARK FOR A NEW GENERATION OF MODERN BALLPARKS.

Overcoming the villainy of Brooklyn's initial move, O'Malley has emerged from history as a pioneer and visionary for expanding baseball's geographic boundaries. Considered a dramatic, bold, and shocking move at the time, it is impossible to deny its success, not only for the team, but for professional baseball as well. A New York City native, O'Malley first became affiliated with the Dodgers when he was appointed the team's attorney after the resignation of Larry MacPhail in 1942, and he purchased a minority interest in the team in November 1944. The death of co-owner John L. Smith in July 1950 and the expiration of Branch Rickey's contract the following October allowed O'Malley to gain controlling interest, which lasted until his passing in 1979. He was elected in 2008.

O'Malley (left) boards a plane at New York's LaGuardia Airport along with Giants' owner Horace Stoneham (right) to attend a National League meeting during the 1957 season. At the meeting, the owners permitted them to move their teams to Los Angeles and San Francisco. At the time, Stoneham was considering a move to Minneapolis until O'Malley convinced him to continue their teams' ongoing rivalry in California.

On April 18, 1958, before 78,672 fans, Walter O'Malley's dream of moving west came true when the LA Dodgers played their first home game, defeating the San Francisco Giants 6-5. Duke Snider produced their first hit with a first-inning single, and his third-inning single plated their first run. They set a new franchise attendance record, drawing 1,845,556 to the coliseum despite finishing in seventh place.

WALTER EMMONS ALSTON

SOFT-SPOKEN, LOW-PROFILE ORGANIZATION MAN WHO MANAGED THE DODGERS FOR 23 YEARS, LEADING TEAM TO ITS ONLY WORLD CHAMPIONSHIP IN BROOKLYN IN 1955 AND TO PENNANT IN 1956 BEFORE TEAM MOVED TO WEST COAST. IN LOS ANGELES HIS CLUBS WON WORLD TITLES IN 1959, 1963 AND 1965 AND PENNANTS IN 1966 AND 1974; AND ONLY JOHN McGRAW, WITH 10, TOPPED ALSTON'S SEVEN N.L. PENNANTS. TEAMS FINISHED IN FIRST DIVISION 18 TIMES, WINNING 2,040 GAMES.

On the last day of the 1936 season, St. Louis Cardinal Walter Alston played in his only MLB game, replacing hall-of-famer Frankie Frisch at first, who had pinch-hit for hall-of-famer Johnny Mize. He played two innings, striking out to end the game. Alston took a decidedly different path to reunite with Mize and Frisch in Cooperstown, beginning with a 1944 managerial job in Brooklyn's minor-league system. While his playing career was but a blink of an eye, his managerial tenure with the Dodgers was the longest and most successful of any in franchise history. Promoted to Brooklyn in 1954, Alston embarked on a remarkable 23 seasons, piloting the Dodgers to seven pennants and four world championships. He was elected in 1983.

"Next year" finally arrived for Dem Bums and their fans on October 4, 1955, when Brooklyn clinched its first World Series title with a 2-0 shutout over the dreaded Yankees. In his second season as skipper, the 43-year-old Walter Alston (No. 24) forever endeared himself in the minds and hearts of the Dodger faithful, delivering the franchise's only world championship while in Brooklyn.

Walter Alston's Dodgers followed up their legendary 1955 campaign with another pennant in 1956 but, once again, fell to the Yankees in the World Series. In 1958, the Dodgers headed west, where Alston began a 19-season span in which he oversaw five National League pennants and three world championships. Alston endeared himself to owner O'Malley not only by winning, but also by signing 23 one-year contracts.

DONALD SCOTT DRYSDALE

BROOKLYN N.L. 1956-1957
LOS ANGELES N.L. 1958-1969

HARD-THROWING SIDE-ARMER NOTED FOR
INTIMIDATING STYLE AND DURABILITY. HAD 209-166
RECORD WITH 2.95 ERA AND 2,486 STRIKEOUTS.
LED N.L. IN STRIKEOUTS 3 TIMES AND HURLED 49
SHUTOUTS. WAS 25-9 IN 1962 AND WON CY YOUNG
AWARD. THREW 6 SHUTOUTS IN A ROW IN 1968,
SETTING RECORD WITH 58 CONSECUTIVE SCORELESS
INNINGS. PITCHED IN RECORD 8 ALL-STAR GAMES.

At six feet, five inches and 190 pounds, Don Drysdale was a fearsome presence on the mound. A soft-spoken gentleman with a reputation for throwing inside, he would downplay those who spoke of him as an intimidator. However, opponents never leaned over the plate and rarely got too comfortable in the box. Drysdale led the NL in hit batsmen five times, including four in a row. He was elected in 1984.

Sandy Koufax (left) and Don Drysdale (right) pitched together for 11 seasons and combined for 340 wins, 75 shutouts, lead the league in strikeouts 6 times, and won 7 of the 12 Dodgers' World Series victories in 1959, 1963, and 1965. In 1966, they executed a joint holdout, threatening to leave baseball for Hollywood. They ultimately agreed to terms that made them the second- (Koufax) and third-highest paid players in the game.

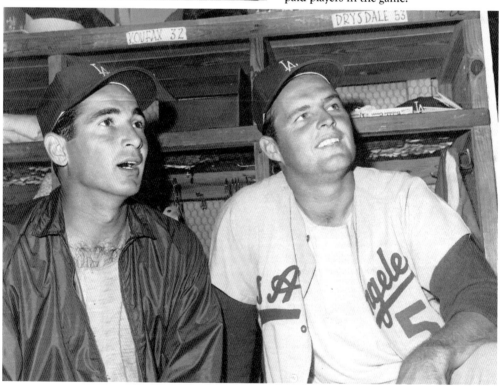

They could not have been more different. Roy Campanella was the product of a mixed marriage that took place when his mother and father ran away to tie the knot in 1907. He grew up with three siblings in a row house in Nicetown, Pennsylvania. Don Drysdale was raised with one sister in the comfortable Los Angeles suburb of Van Nuys. Drysdale, the 20-year-old phenom, and Campy, the grizzled veteran catcher, met in Brooklyn. Campanella caught Drysdale's debut, his first strikeout, first win, and first shutout. However, he never got to wear the "LA" on his cap while Drysdale flourished in his hometown. The 71-year-old Campy died of a heart attack, and Drysdale attended his funeral on June 30, 1993. Just three days later, a heart attack claimed the 56-year-old Drysdale as well.

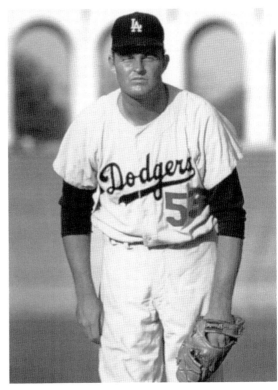

On June 4, 1968, Don Drysdale pitched at Dodger Stadium, and Robert F. Kennedy won California's presidential primary. Kennedy opened his victory speech with "I want to express my high regard to Don Drysdale, who pitched his sixth straight shutout . . . I hope we have as good fortune." Minutes later, Kennedy was shot. On the night Drysdale died, a cassette tape of that speech was found on the nightstand of his hotel room, forever connecting them in life and death.

Don Drysdale and teammate Pee Wee Reese were members of the induction class of 1984. Drysdale said, "Thanksgiving comes early in 1984. . . . To ever think that I would be sitting today at the autograph session between Happy Chandler and Charlie Gehringer . . . was complete fantasyland." In closing, he saluted the fans: "If not for you . . . walking through turnstiles, turning on radios, turning on televisions . . . baseball would not survive."

GOODBYE, FLATBUSH; HELLO, HOLLYWOOD

Coming out of spring training in 1966, Dodger manager Walter Alston inserted 21-year-old rookie Don Sutton in the starting rotation of the defending world champions. Working in the shadow of Sandy Koufax and Don Drysdale, the youngster showed remarkable poise and potential in his 35 starts. His 209 strikeouts were the most by a National League rookie since hall-of-famer Grover Cleveland Alexander threw 227 in 1911. An arm injury kept him out of the World Series, a losing effort against Baltimore. Tremendously durable and consistent, Sutton spent the first 15 years of his career with the Dodgers en route to 324 career wins. His 756 career starts rank third all-time behind fellow Cooperstown greats Cy Young and Nolan Ryan. The only Dodger-bred pitcher to accumulate 300-plus wins, Sutton was elected in 1998.

DONALD HOWARD SUTTON

LOS ANGELES, N.L., 1966-80, 1988
HOUSTON, N.L., 1981-82
MILWAUKEE, A.L., 1982-84
OAKLAND, A.L., 1985
CALIFORNIA, A.L., 1985-1987

A STALWART ON THE MOUND FOR 23 MAJOR LEAGUE SEASONS, HIS IMPRESSIVE PITCHING RECORD INCLUDES 324 VICTORIES, 3,574 STRIKEOUTS AND A 3.26 ERA. STRIKEOUT TOTAL IS FIFTH BEST ALL-TIME, WHILE WIN TOTAL RANKS TIED FOR 12th. DID NOT MISS A TURN IN THE STARTING ROTATION DUE TO INJURY OR ILLNESS. CONSISTENCY AND MODEL CONTROL LED TO 15 OR MORE WINS IN 12 SEASONS AND 100 OR MORE STRIKEOUTS 21 TIMES. THE RIGHT-HANDER PITCHED IN FOUR WORLD SERIES AND WAS NAMED TO FOUR ALL-STAR TEAMS.

During a five-year stretch beginning in 1972, the remarkably consistent Don Sutton averaged 18 wins while appearing in four All-Star Games, in which he allowed zero runs while striking out seven. Sutton returned to the Dodgers in 1988 for his final season and recorded his final career victory in Dodger blue. His 3,574 career strikeouts remain seventh-most of all time.

In 1982, Don Sutton told *Sports Illustrated*, "Other kids were playing for fun, I was playing to get to the big leagues." In his hall of fame induction speech in 1998, Don recalled his mother worrying about the imaginary childhood friends he played baseball with: "She didn't know a Mickey, or a Whitey, or a Yogi, or a Moose, or an Elston, but I played with them every day." Sutton is now a permanent member of the team.

After Dodger pitcher Don Drysdale retired in August 1969, the team made a trade with Pittsburgh for experienced veteran starter Jim Bunning. The Dodgers, only two games out of first place with 46 games to play, were hopeful Bunning could help keep them in the West Division race. The nine-time All-Star was an extremely tough competitor and a 20-game winner who had won 19 games on four other occasions. In 1964, Bunning threw a perfect game, the first in the National League since 1880. At the time of the trade, only Walter Johnson had struck out more batters in the 20th century than Bunning's total of 2,617. He went 3-1 with the Dodgers, who ultimately finished in fourth place. After retirement, he served several terms as a US congressman and senator. Bunning was elected in 1996.

JAMES HOYT WILHELM
NEW YORK N.L., 1952-1956 ST. LOUIS N.L., 1957
CLEVELAND A.L., 1957-1958 BALTIMORE A.L., 1958-1962
CHICAGO A.L., 1963-1968 CALIFORNIA A.L., 1969
ATLANTA N.L., 1969-1970, 1971 CHICAGO N.L., 1970
LOS ANGELES N.L., 1971-1972
BASEBALL'S PREMIER RELIEF PITCHER. USED KNUCKLE
BALL TO WIN 143 GAMES (A RECORD 124 IN RELIEF)
AND AMASSED 227 SAVES OVER 21-YEAR CAREER.
NO-HIT YANKEES ON SEPT. 20, 1958 IN INFREQUENT
START FOR ORIOLES. PITCHED IN RECORD 1070
GAMES WITH LIFETIME ERA OF 2.52.

In 1944, Hoyt Wilhelm's career almost ended before it started at World War II's decisive Battle of the Bulge. Wilhelm was awarded a Purple Heart for wounds sustained and played his entire career with a piece of shrapnel in his back. He was 29 years old when he made his major-league debut, and he was the first-ever relief pitcher to be enshrined in Cooperstown. He was elected in 1985.

Hall-of-famer Brooks Robinson once said of Wilhelm, "He had the best knuckleball you'd ever want to see," and by his 20th season, the 48 year old had established himself as the most effective pure knuckleball pitcher in baseball history. Wilhelm finished his career in Los Angeles in 1972, earning his then major-league-record 228th and final save, in his first appearance on April 17. He was released on July 21, five days before his 50th birthday.

In December 1971, the Dodgers acquired Frank Robinson. The 36 year old had just led Baltimore to their third-straight World Series, and he was still an All-Star. The two-time MVP had slugged his 500th career home run in September, becoming the 11th member of that exclusive club. The 10th player to win the Triple Crown in baseball's modern era, Frank Robinson was elected in 1982.

FRANK ROBINSON

CINCINNATI N.L., BALTIMORE A.L.,
LOS ANGELES N.L., CALIFORNIA A.L.,
CLEVELAND A.L., 1956-1976
FIRST TO BE CHOSEN MOST VALUABLE PLAYER
IN BOTH LEAGUES -- N.L. IN 1961 AND A.L.
IN 1966. SET RECORDS BY HITTING HOMERS
IN 32 DIFFERENT PARKS AND WITH PAIR OF
GRAND-SLAMMERS IN SUCCESSIVE INNINGS IN
1970. FOURTH IN HOMERS (586), FIFTH IN
EXTRA BASES ON LONG HITS (2,430), SIXTH
IN TOTAL BASES (5,373), ON RETIRING. LED
N.L. IN SLUGGING PCT. IN 1960-61-62 AND
A.L. IN BATTING, HOMERS, RUNS BATTED IN,
TOTAL BASES AND SLUGGING PCT. IN 1966.

In his only season with the Dodgers, he played his usual right field position, batted clean-up, and swatted 19 home runs. In 1975, when Frank Robinson was hired to manage the Cleveland Indians, he fulfilled Jackie Robinson's hope to "look at that third base coaching line one day and see a Black face managing in baseball." Sadly, Jackie was not here to see it. Frank Robinson managed 16 seasons with the Indians, Giants, Orioles, Expos, and Nationals.

JUAN ANTONIO
MARICHAL SANCHEZ

SAN FRANCISCO N. L., 1960-1973 BOSTON A. L. 1974
LOS ANGELES N. L., 1975
HIGH-KICKING RIGHT-HANDER FROM DOMINICAN
REPUBLIC WON 243 GAMES AND LOST ONLY 142
OVER 16 SEASONS. WON 20 GAMES SIX TIMES AND
NO-HIT HOUSTON IN 1963. LED N.L. IN COMPLETE
GAMES AND SHUTOUTS TWICE AND IN ERA WITH
2.10 IN 1969. COMPLETED 244 GAMES DURING
CAREER, STRIKING OUT 2,303 AND FINISHING
WITH 2.89 ERA.

Juan Marichal signed with the Dodgers because, in his words, "I wanted them to get to know me." Ten years earlier, he was involved in one of baseball's darkest incidents. In the midst of a "dust off" battle with the Giants, Marichal clubbed Dodger catcher John Roseboro with his bat, opening a gash in his head that required 14 stitches to close. Roseboro and Marichal would eventually reconcile, and their families became friends. For Marichal's first two years on the BBWAA ballot, he did not receive enough votes to be enshrined. Roseboro (below, left) made a personal appeal to the BBWAA to not hold the "incident" against him. He was inducted the following year. Marichal (below, right) delivered the eulogy at Roseboro's funeral and said that John forgiving him was "one of the best things that ever happened in his life."

THE LEFT ARM OF GOD

He was born Sanford Braun in Brooklyn in December 1935, when Casey Stengel was managing the Dodgers and Dazzy Vance had just completed the last year of his 16-year hall of fame career. His parents divorced when he was just three, and when he was nine, his mom married Irving Koufax, the man whom Sandy would come to call "dad." They moved to Long Island, but after Sandy finished the ninth grade, they were back in Brooklyn, where he attended Lafayette High School and played basketball.

A high school basketball standout, he played only one year of baseball. His basketball prowess earned him a walk-on opportunity at the University of Cincinnati, and he joined the baseball team because he heard they were going to New Orleans. "I'd never been to New Orleans, so I decided I'd probably be a pretty good baseball player, maybe," Sandy told ESPN.

In 1955, at the age of 19, he was a Brooklyn Dodger, a "bonus baby" signing for $4,000. Surrounded by Reese, Hodges, Robinson, Snider, and Campanella, all destined for Cooperstown, he was on a pitching staff headed by Don Newcombe, the 1949 Rookie of the Year. Newcombe won the 1956 MVP award and Cy Young Award, becoming the first pitcher to win both in the same season. As the young lefty took his place among these giants of the game, he did so with precisely 31 innings of college pitching experience. The rules regarding bonus babies were such that he could not be sent to the minors, and thus, Koufax had to learn his craft while playing at the highest level.

In his first six years, he struggled with command and control. In 103 starts, he completed 22 of them, going 36-40 with an opponent's batting average against of .225. He struck out 8.9 batters per nine innings and walked 5.3. His average year was 6-7 with a 4.10 ERA. Yet within the erraticism were flashes of spectacular brilliance and astonishing dominance.

Then came a spring training road trip to Tinker Field in Orlando in March 1961. The *Orlando Sentinel* reported, "The Dodgers . . . left nearly all of their regulars back home in Vero Beach." This set the stage for an event that would transform Sandy Koufax. His catcher that day, Norm Sherry, in a 2016 interview with Hillel Kuttler of the Jewish Baseball Museum, recalled the tale: "He couldn't throw a strike, and he ended up walking the first three guys. I went to the mound and said, 'Sandy, we don't have many guys here; we're going to be here a long day. Why don't you take something off the ball and just put it in there.' . . . Good God! He tried to ease up, and he was throwing harder than when he tried to . . . he got his rhythm better, and the ball jumped out of his hand and exploded at the plate." That performance unleashed six seasons of dominance unparalleled in baseball history.

He completed 115 of his 211 starts going 129-47, throwing 35 shutouts—four of them no-hitters and one a perfect game. His opponent's batting average against was .197, and he struck out 9.4 batters per nine innings and walked only 2.3. His average year was 22-8, with an ERA of 2.19. He was the first man to win three Cy Young Awards (when there was only one winner each year), the first man to throw four no-hitters, and the first man to strike out 300-plus in a season three times. He led the league in ERA five years in a row and strikeouts four times, and in 1963, he joined Newcombe, winning the Cy Young Award and MVP award in the same season—the "Left Arm of God," indeed.

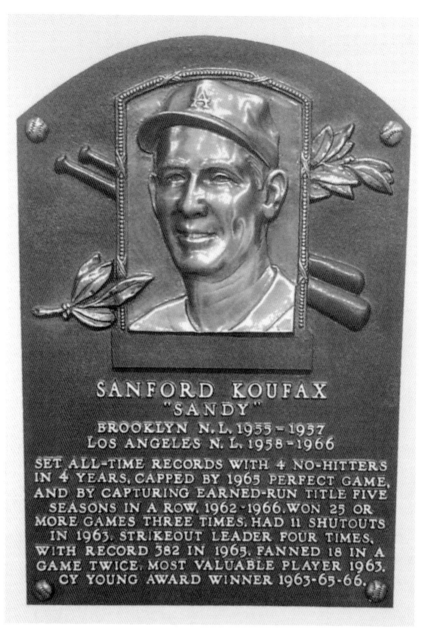

SANFORD KOUFAX
"SANDY"
BROOKLYN N.L. 1955-1957
LOS ANGELES N.L. 1958-1966
SET ALL-TIME RECORDS WITH 4 NO-HITTERS
IN 4 YEARS, CAPPED BY 1965 PERFECT GAME,
AND BY CAPTURING EARNED-RUN TITLE FIVE
SEASONS IN A ROW, 1962-1966. WON 25 OR
MORE GAMES THREE TIMES. HAD 11 SHUTOUTS
IN 1963. STRIKEOUT LEADER FOUR TIMES,
WITH RECORD 382 IN 1965. FANNED 18 IN A
GAME TWICE. MOST VALUABLE PLAYER 1963.
CY YOUNG AWARD WINNER 1963-65-66.

In 1972, at the age of 36, Sandy Koufax was the youngest man to achieve the honor of being inducted into the hall of fame. He received 86 percent of the writer's votes his first time on the ballot. His final season was in 1966, which he shared with 21-year-old rookie right-hander Don Sutton, who would join him in the hall of fame in 1998. In a 1999 ESPN interview, Sutton summarized the career of Koufax: "Greg Maddux is a remarkable artist, Bob Gibson was a dominator, Tom Seaver was outstanding, Carlton, magnificent. The man who stands alone as the most dominating pitcher I ever saw, without a doubt and with no equal, was Sandy Koufax." As the 2023 season begins, he has been a hall of famer for a half-century, and he has led his life with a dignified humility that makes him one of the most revered sports figures in American history.

Sandy Koufax threw only 31 innings for the Bearcats and went 3-1 with a 2.88 ERA, striking out 51 batters and walking 30. He had 18 strikeouts (a school record) against Louisville. In his first professional outing, an intra-squad game in March 1955, he pitched two innings, striking out five and walking two. Nobody put the ball in play, as the third out of his second inning ended on a "strike 'em out, throw 'em out."

Sandy Koufax's first win came on August 27, 1955, at Ebbets Field, in a 7-0 two-hit shutout with 14 strikeouts (the NL season high) against the Reds. Here, he is congratulated by Roy Campanella (No. 39), Jackie Robinson (No. 42), and Gil Hodges (No. 14). A week later, he shut out the Pirates on five hits. His first two wins were shutouts, surrendering a combined seven hits with 20 strikeouts—a portent for NL hitters. (Charles Hoff.)

From 1956 to 1958, Sandy Koufax pitched 322 innings in 49 starts and 41 relief appearances. He was 18-19, with one save and a 4.36 ERA. He reached double digits in strikeouts only five times. In 1959, his dominance began to emerge. On June 22, he struck out 16 Phillies, establishing a new record for night games. Then, in a 13-day stretch, reeled off three consecutive games of double-digit strikeouts, including tying Bob Feller's MLB record of 18.

Sandy Koufax watched the 1955 and 1956 World Series from the Brooklyn dugout. He made his first World Series start in 1959 before a record 92,706 fans in the Los Angeles Coliseum against the White Sox and Bob Shaw (pictured). In a spectacular pitcher's duel, Shaw and the White Sox prevailed 1-0 as the Dodgers left 11 men on base. The only run scored was on a ground ball double play in the fourth inning.

THE LEFT ARM OF GOD

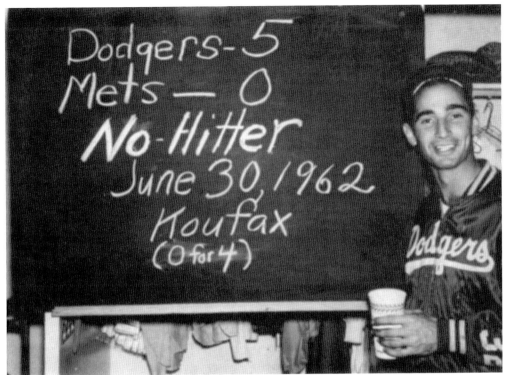

During 1960 and 1961, Sandy Koufax gained command, and more flashes of his future self emerged. Those flashes became the norm in 1962. In his first 21 starts, he was 14-4 with a 2.06 ERA and nine double-digit strikeout games, including punching out 18 Cubs in April. He hurled his first no-hitter, which came in a stretch of eight games where he pitched 54 innings and went 6-2 with a 0.67 ERA and 77 strikeouts. A finger injury virtually ended his season in mid-July.

In 1963, the Left Arm of God arrived in Los Angeles, California, as Sandy Koufax totally dominated the league. He was an astounding 25-5 with a minuscule 1.88 ERA, which was above 2.00 for a total of only 14 days all season. His fourth win was his second no-hitter, an 8-0 win against the Giants at Dodger Stadium. He joined his old teammate and mentor Don Newcombe in winning the Cy Young Award and MVP award.

From 1947 through 1956, the Brooklyn Dodgers and New York Yankees faced off in six World Series. The 1963 series marked the first rematch since 1956. Koufax pitched game one, beating the Yankees while striking out 15 of them, including the first five in order. In Mickey Mantle's first at-bat, in which he was called out on strikes, he turned to catcher John Roseboro and said, "How the fuck are you supposed to hit that stuff?"

Sandy Koufax's 15 strikeouts set a new World Series record, breaking that of Dodger Carl Erskine (right) who, 10 years earlier to the day, struck out 14 Yankees in the 1953 World Series. Mickey Mantle fell victim to both pitchers. Koufax and Erskine, along with Roger Craig, are the surviving members of the 1955 world champion Dodgers. As the 2023 season begins, Koufax is the youngster at 87, Carl Erskine is 96, and Roger Craig is 93.

THE LEFT ARM OF GOD

Sandy Koufax was called upon in game four, and he completed the sweep with a 2-1 complete game win. The World Series was the crowning jewel in his year of dominance; he was named the 1963 World Series MVP, going 2-0 with a 1.50 ERA. The Dodgers winning pitchers in the series—Koufax, Don Drysdale, and Johnny Podres—all began in Brooklyn, sweetening the taste of this win. Maury Wills (No. 30) runs to join Koufax and catcher Johnny Roseboro in celebration.

The dominance continued in 1964 but was cut short by his arthritic left elbow. He went 19-5, and his ERA dropped to 1.74. He reached double digits in strikeouts 10 times and threw his third no-hitter in three years, a 3-0 win, with 12 strikeouts against the Phillies. His last outing came on August 16, with a 3-0, thirteen-strikeout performance against the Cardinals. His elbow became enflamed and ended his season.

On September 9, 1965, Sandy Koufax threw his fourth no-hitter, a perfect game against the Cubs, beginning a streak of brilliance that led the Dodgers to the NL pennant. In six starts, he was 5-1 with a save. He pitched 52 innings, striking out 61, walking nine, and allowing but 20 hits and two earned runs for a 0.35 ERA. His three hitter against the Braves on October 2 clinched the pennant.

Sandy Koufax did not open the 1965 World Series because it fell on Yom Kippur, giving Don Drysdale (right) the start. "It was no hard decision," Sandy related decades later, "It was a matter of respect, I wasn't trying to make a statement, and I had no idea it would effect so many people." After the Dodgers' loss in game one, Drysdale quipped to Walter Alston, "I bet you wish I was Jewish too."

THE LEFT ARM OF GOD

Sandy Koufax lost game two and then pitched game five with the series tied, taking 112 pitches to shut out the Twins on four hits while striking out 10. With only two days of rest, he hurled game seven as well (seen here) using 132 pitches and throwing a three-hit shutout, once again striking out 10. The Dodgers were world champs for the second time in three years and the fourth time in 10.

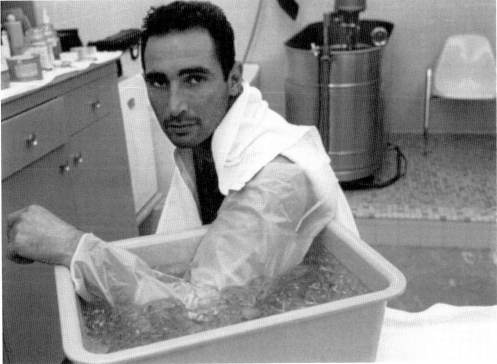

Sandy Koufax suffered from "traumatic arthritis" in his pitching elbow causing him to, what Don Sutton observed, "Not only pitch in pain but rest in pain as well." Major League Baseball Players Association (MLBPA) head Marvin Miller met Koufax at the 1966 All-Star Game when he was soaking his arm in ice. "I'd never seen an arm swollen so badly," he recalled, "and when he saw the alarm on my face, he said, 'Don't worry, it always does this after I pitch.' "

In 1966, Sandy Koufax (left) led the NL in 11 pitching categories, including 27 wins, setting the modern record for seasonal wins by an NL lefty, a record he still shares. His final appearance came in game two of the 1966 World Series, where he fell victim to poor defense and Baltimore's 20-year-old Jim Palmer (right). Palmer threw a four-hit shutout as the Orioles swept the Dodgers. Six weeks later, Koufax's retirement shook the baseball world.

In November 1966, 30-year-old Koufax announced his retirement. "Too many shots, and too many pills," he said, referring to coping with his arthritic left elbow. "I don't regret . . . the 12 years I've spent in baseball, but I could regret one season too many." Koufax turned prophetic when he said, "I've got a lot of years to live after baseball, and I'd like to live them with the complete use of my body." On December 30, 2022, he turned 87.

8

LASORDA'S DODGER TOWN

When Sandy Koufax retired following the 1966 season, he took with him Dodger dominance. The Dodgers had captured 10 NL pennants and four world championships in 20 years. The Divisional Series arrived in 1969, and the road to the World Series became a multistep process. It would take the Dodgers eight years to return to the Fall Classic, a five-game loss to the Oakland A's, who captured their third-straight world championship. In the third base box during that World Series was Thomas Charles Lasorda, named to that position the year before by Walter Alston, the man he would replace in 1976.

Lasorda was 17 years old when he signed with the Phillies in January 1945. Pitching in the Class C Canadian American League for the Schenectady Blue Jays in June 1948, he struck out 25 in a 15-inning complete game win against Amsterdam. In 1949, the Dodgers drafted him from the Phillies and assigned him to their class A team in Greenville, South Carolina. This began an affiliation with the Dodgers, which, save for one year, would last until his passing in January 2021. His major-league career consisted of 58.33 innings pitched in which he was 0-4, with one save and an ERA of 6.48. He played 14 years in the minor leagues, four under the tutelage of Walter Alston. In 1965, he began an eight-year stretch of managing in the Dodgers' system; the last four years were with the Dodgers AAA affiliate in the Pacific Coast League.

Lasorda embarked on a new trend for baseball managers: socializing with his players. He felt it fostered loyalty, which could only strengthen the team. Mark Guthrie, a 15-year left-handed relief specialist, spent four years under Lasorda. He recalled, "He knew my wife's name, my kids' names, and often asked about them. . . . You'd be walking about a city on the road, he'd spot you, flag you down, and take you to lunch . . . usually an Italian restaurant. . . . Tommy was a great guy." No Dodger was more loyal than Tommy Lasorda, who always said he "bled Dodger blue" and wanted to be buried under the pitcher's mound at Dodger Stadium.

The Dodgers won the World Series in 1988 under Lasorda, upsetting a heavily favored Oakland A's team in five games, and he was named NL Manager of the Year for the second time. Nearly three decades passed before they returned to the Fall Classic, losing in 2017 and again in 2018 before recapturing the brass ring by defeating the Tampa Bay Rays in 2020.

Throughout Lasorda's tenure, only five players wore his beloved Dodger blue on their own personal march to Cooperstown. Three of them arrived via the Dodgers farm system, and two would achieve their ultimate glory in other uniforms. One left via free agency, and the other was traded away.

The arrival of the new millennia brought four of the game's true all-time greats to Dodger Stadium, each at the end of an illustrious career. In 2022, the Dodgers turned their eyes back three-quarters of a century, remembering those thrilling days of yesteryear as they celebrated Gil Hodges joining his mates in what Branch Rickey called the "sanctum sanctorum of the game," Cooperstown's hallowed halls.

THOMAS CHARLES LASORDA

LOS ANGELES, N.L., 1977-1996

ONE OF BASEBALL'S MOST ENGAGING PERSONALITIES
AND A GREAT AMBASSADOR FOR HIS SPORT, MANAGED
DODGERS WITH AN IMPENETRABLE PASSION, CLAIMING
TO "BLEED DODGER BLUE." IN HIS 47TH SEASON
WITH THE DODGERS ORGANIZATION WHEN HE RETIRED
AS MANAGER. FOURTH MANAGER IN HISTORY TO
GUIDE SAME FRANCHISE FOR 20 YEARS. DURING
WHICH HE WON EIGHT DIVISION TITLES, FOUR N.L.
PENNANTS AND WORLD CHAMPIONSHIPS IN 1981 AND
1988. 61 POST-SEASON GAMES MANAGED RANKS THIRD
MOST IN HISTORY.

In nine seasons with the Montreal Royals, Tommy Lasorda won a franchise record 107 games, and he was inducted into the Canadian Baseball Hall of Fame in 2006. He had one start with the major-league Dodgers. It lasted one inning, in which he walked two, threw three wild pitches, and struck out two. From that inauspicious Dodger career, Lasorda became one of the most beloved Dodgers of all time. He was elected in 1997.

Tommy Lasorda (standing) is seen here at a press conference after replacing Walter Alston (left) as Dodger manager in September 1976. Lasorda piloted the Dodgers to back-to-back NL pennants in 1977 and 1978 and again in 1981, this time capturing the World Series, the Dodgers' first since 1965. Combined, Alston and Lasorda steered the Dodgers for 43 seasons, winning 11 pennants and six World Series. (Photograph by Dave Smith.)

Lasorda and Kirk Gibson shared one of baseball's most iconic moments in game one of the 1988 World Series against Dennis Eckersley and the Oakland A's. Hobbled by multiple leg injuries and barely able to walk, Gibson gingerly limped to home plate with two outs in the bottom of the ninth. "I'd never seen such a reception," Lasorda recalled. "I got goosebumps just listening to the roar of the crowd." He hit a two-run homer, ending the game. "In a year that has been so improbable, the impossible has happened," came the Dodgers' hall of fame broadcaster Vin Scully's iconic call. And then silence before Dodger Stadium erupted. Two weeks later, the team visited the White House. Lasorda stands between Pres. Ronald Reagan and World Series MVP Orel Hershiser.

EDDIE CLARENCE MURRAY
BALTIMORE, A.L., 1977-1988, 1996
LOS ANGELES, N.L., 1989-1991, 1997
NEW YORK, N.L., 1992-1993
CLEVELAND, A.L., 1994-1996
ANAHEIM, A.L., 1997
A POWERFUL AND PRODUCTIVE SWITCH-HITTER WHOSE CONSISTENCY OVER
21 SEASONS LED TO 3,255 HITS, 560 DOUBLES, 504 HOME RUNS, 5,397 TOTAL
BASES, AND 1,917 RBI. THIRD PLAYER EVER TO CONNECT FOR MORE THAN 500
HOME RUNS AND 3,000 HITS. PLAYED IN THREE WORLD SERIES, WINNING
WITH THE ORIOLES IN 1983. AN EIGHT-TIME ALL-STAR AND THE 1977 AL
ROOKIE OF THE YEAR. A SKILLED FIELDER, HE EARNED THREE GOLD GLOVE
AWARDS, SETTING MAJOR LEAGUE RECORDS FOR GAMES PLAYED AND
ASSISTS BY A FIRST BASEMAN.

In closing his 13-minute hall of fame induction speech, Lasorda summed up what it all meant to him: "Growing up, I was a Yankee fan. . . . I used to actually dream I was pitching for the Yankees. . . . Bill Dickey was giving me the signs. . . . I'd feel my mother shaking me. . . . Wake up, Tommy, it's time to go to school. . . . The hall of fame is eternity, and I thank God for all of it. . . . I am living a dream, thank you."

Cal Ripken Jr. once said, "When I got to the big leagues, there was a man—Eddie Murray—who showed me how to play this game, day in and day out. I thank him for his example." The eight-time All-Star is the all-time leader in games played at first base (2,413) and became the third player in history, joining legends Hank Aaron and Willie Mays, to record both 3,000 hits and 500 home runs. He was elected in 2003.

Six weeks after winning the 1988 World Series, the Dodgers upgraded their roster by acquiring Orioles superstar Eddie Murray. The Los Angeles native, who was still in his prime, brought with him 333 home runs, 1,190 runs batted in, three Gold Gloves, a world championship, and a Rookie of the Year award. His highest single-season average (.330) came in a Dodger uniform.

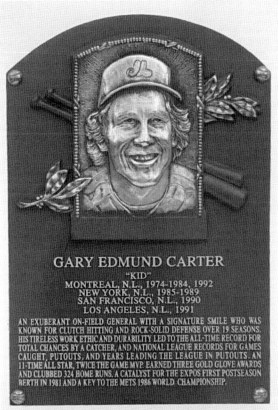

GARY EDMUND CARTER
"KID"
MONTREAL, N.L., 1974-1984, 1992
NEW YORK, N.L., 1985-1989
SAN FRANCISCO, N.L., 1990
LOS ANGELES, N.L., 1991

AN EXUBERANT ON-FIELD GENERAL WITH A SIGNATURE SMILE WHO WAS KNOWN FOR CLUTCH HITTING AND ROCK-SOLID DEFENSE OVER 19 SEASONS. HIS TIRELESS WORK ETHIC AND DURABILITY LED TO THE ALL-TIME RECORD FOR TOTAL CHANCES BY A CATCHER, AND NATIONAL LEAGUE RECORDS FOR GAMES CAUGHT, PUTOUTS, AND YEARS LEADING THE LEAGUE IN PUTOUTS. AN 11-TIME ALL STAR, TWICE THE GAME MVP. EARNED THREE GOLD GLOVE AWARDS AND CLUBBED 324 HOME RUNS. A CATALYST FOR THE EXPOS FIRST POSTSEASON BERTH IN 1981 AND A KEY TO THE METS 1986 WORLD CHAMPIONSHIP.

By the early 1980s, Gary Carter was regarded as the finest all-around catcher in baseball. The 1975 NL Rookie of the Year landed on 11 National League All-Star teams and twice won the game's MVP award. He slugged 25-plus home runs five times, had 100-plus RBI four times, and won three Gold Glove Awards. He was elected in 2003.

In 1986, Gary Carter ignited a game six come-from-behind victory in the World Series, catapulting the Mets to the championship. In early 1991, Carter was unsigned when Dodger manager Tommy Lasorda invited him to spring training. He won a job with Los Angeles, and he got his 2,000th hit and scored his 1,000th run in one season with the Dodgers.

MICHAEL JOSEPH PIAZZA
"MIKE"
LOS ANGELES, N.L., 1992-98; FLORIDA, N.L., 1998; NEW YORK, N.L., 1998-2005; SAN DIEGO, N.L., 2006; OAKLAND, A.L., 2007

A DURABLE AND PROLIFIC POWER-HITTING CATCHER WHO BELTED 427 CAREER HOME RUNS, INCLUDING A RECORD 396 AT THE POSITION. CAUGHT AT LEAST 100 GAMES 11 TIMES, LEADING N.L. IN PUTOUTS ON FOUR OCCASIONS. THE 1993 N.L. ROOKIE OF THE YEAR AND A 12-TIME ALL-STAR, NAMED GAME MVP IN 1996. LED METS TO THE 2000 SUBWAY SERIES, AND HELPED RALLY A NATION ONE YEAR LATER WITH HIS DRAMATIC HOME RUN IN THE FIRST METS GAME IN NEW YORK FOLLOWING THE 9/11 ATTACKS.

As a favor to Mike Piazza's dad, a childhood friend, Tommy Lasorda made Piazza the 1,390th overall pick of the 1988 amateur draft. Lasorda convinced the first baseman to switch to catcher, improving his chances of making it to the majors. The move worked, as Piazza retired as the all-time home run leader among catchers. The lowest draft pick to reach Cooperstown, he was elected in 2016.

Piazza made his Dodgers debut on September 1, 1992, and the following spring, he was named the starting catcher. He began the 1993 season with an 11-game hitting streak en route to setting a home run record for rookie catchers (35) while running away with the Rookie of the Year award. In five full seasons with the Dodgers, Piazza's average year was .337, with 33 home runs and 105 RBI.

In his five Dodger seasons, he was an All-Star five times and was well on his way to becoming one of the greatest hitting catchers in history. In 1997, he became the first player to record 200 hits in a season while appearing in at least 100 games as a catcher. Piazza thrilled the Mets home crowd in 2001 by homering in the city's first game after the September 11 attacks.

PEDRO JAIME MARTÍNEZ
LOS ANGELES, N.L. 1992-93; MONTREAL, N.L. 1994-97;
BOSTON, A.L. 1998-2004; NEW YORK, N.L. 2005-08;
PHILADELPHIA, N.L. 2009

FEATURING AN ELECTRIC ARSENAL OF PITCHES THAT VANQUISHED
BATTERS DURING AN ERA OF HIGH OCTANE OFFENSE, THE FIERY
RIGHTY FROM THE DOMINICAN REPUBLIC OWNED THE INSIDE PART OF
THE PLATE WITH AN EXPLODING FASTBALL AND CONFOUNDING
CHANGE-UP. LED LEAGUE IN E.R.A. FIVE TIMES AND STRIKEOUTS
THREE TIMES EN ROUTE TO THREE CY YOUNG AWARDS AND EIGHT ALL-
STAR SELECTIONS. FIRST PITCHER TO RETIRE WITH 3,154 STRIKEOUTS
IN FEWER THAN 3,000 INNINGS. WON 219 GAMES WITH AN ASTOUNDING
.687 WINNING PERCENTAGE. POSTED 117-37 RECORD IN BOSTON,
HELPING TO LEAD RED SOX TO 2004 WORLD SERIES CHAMPIONSHIP.

When Pedro Martinez made his debut with the Dodgers in September 1992, he was known as the "kid" brother of the team's star pitcher Ramon Martinez. Pitching out of the bullpen his rookie year, Pedro went 10-5 with a 2.61 ERA and had 10 strikeouts per nine innings pitched. Despite his success, the Dodgers had doubts about the durability of his 5-foot, 11-inch, 170-pound frame and traded him to the Expos. Pedro blossomed, winning his first Cy Young Award in 1997. He added two more Cy Youngs with the Red Sox (1999 and 2000) and, in 2004, became a world champion. Ramon reunited with Pedro in Boston, where the younger Martinez was blazing a trail to baseball's hall of fame and where Ramon was known as Pedro's "big" brother. Pedro was elected in 2015.

After a 24-year big-league career, Rickey Henderson loved playing baseball too much to stop and began the 2003 season with the Newark Bears in the independent Atlantic League. By midseason, the Dodgers came calling, and Henderson, nicknamed "the Man of Steal," signed on July 14. He arrived with an iron-clad, indisputable hall of fame resume: 3,040 hits and the all-time records for runs scored (2,288), stolen bases (1,403), and unintentional walks (2,126). He successfully stole all three bases he attempted with the Dodgers, ending his career with 1,406, a record that may forever stand. The two-time world champion, 10-time All-Star, and 1990 American League MVP is generally considered the greatest leadoff hitter of all time. Henderson was elected in 2009.

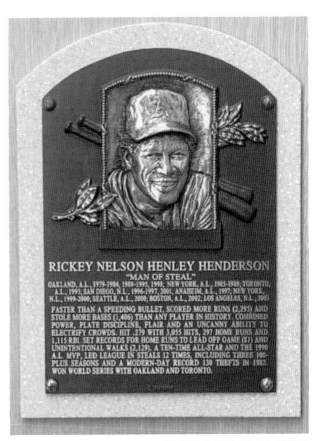

RICKEY NELSON HENLEY HENDERSON
"MAN OF STEAL"
OAKLAND, A.L. 1979-1984, 1989-1995, 1998; NEW YORK, A.L. 1985-1989, TORONTO, A.L. 1993; SAN DIEGO, N.L. 1996-1997, 2001; ANAHEIM, A.L. 1997; NEW YORK, N.L. 1999-2000; SEATTLE, A.L. 2000; BOSTON, A.L. 2002; LOS ANGELES, N.L. 2003

FASTER THAN A SPEEDING BULLET, SCORED MORE RUNS (2,295) AND STOLE MORE BASES (1,406) THAN ANY PLAYER IN HISTORY. COMBINED POWER, PLATE DISCIPLINE, FLAIR AND AN UNCANNY ABILITY TO ELECTRIFY CROWDS. HIT .279 WITH 3,055 HITS, 297 HOME RUNS AND 1,115 RBI. SET RECORDS FOR HOME RUNS TO LEAD OFF GAME (81) AND UNINTENTIONAL WALKS (2,129). A TEN-TIME ALL-STAR AND THE 1990 A.L. MVP. LED LEAGUE IN STEALS 12 TIMES, INCLUDING THREE 100-PLUS SEASONS AND A MODERN-DAY RECORD 130 THEFTS IN 1982. WON WORLD SERIES WITH OAKLAND AND TORONTO.

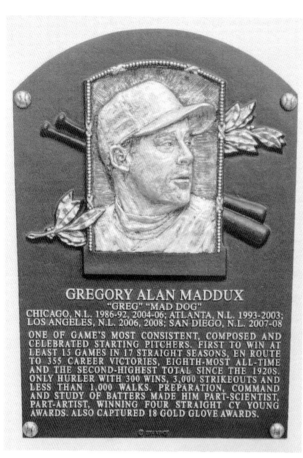

GREGORY ALAN MADDUX
"GREG" "MAD DOG"
CHICAGO, N.L. 1986-92, 2004-06; ATLANTA, N.L. 1993-2003;
LOS ANGELES, N.L. 2006, 2008; SAN DIEGO, N.L. 2007-08
ONE OF GAME'S MOST CONSISTENT, COMPOSED AND
CELEBRATED STARTING PITCHERS. FIRST TO WIN AT
LEAST 15 GAMES IN 17 STRAIGHT SEASONS, EN ROUTE
TO 355 CAREER VICTORIES, EIGHTH-MOST ALL-TIME
AND THE SECOND-HIGHEST TOTAL SINCE THE 1920S.
ONLY HURLER WITH 300 WINS, 3,000 STRIKEOUTS AND
LESS THAN 1,000 WALKS. PREPARATION, COMMAND
AND STUDY OF BATTERS MADE HIM PART-SCIENTIST,
PART-ARTIST. WINNING FOUR STRAIGHT CY YOUNG
AWARDS. ALSO CAPTURED 18 GOLD GLOVE AWARDS.

Forty years old and nearing the end of his spectacular career, Greg Maddux was a welcome addition to the Dodgers at the 2006 trading deadline. The author of one of the most historic pitching careers in baseball, he arrived with 327 victories, 3,133 strikeouts, four straight Cy Young Awards, a world championship, and 18 Gold Gloves—the most since the award's inception in 1957. He is the only pitcher in major-league history to win at least 15 games for 17 consecutive years. Maddux finished the 2006 season with the Dodgers and returned in 2008, recording his 355th and final career victory in September, almost 23 years to the day of his first major-league win. Maddux and longtime teammate Tom Glavine were reunited in 2014 as both were elected to the hall of fame.

The Dodgers added one of the top power hitters in history when they acquired left-handed slugger Jim Thome in late 2009. Arriving in Los Angeles with five All-Star appearances and 564 career home runs, Thome joined a Dodger team that included Manny Ramirez, also a member of the 500 home run club. He is one of only nine men to reach the 600 home run plateau (612), and he joined Barry Bonds, Babe Ruth, Ted Williams, and Mel Ott as the only players with at least 500 home runs, 1,500 runs scored, 1,600 RBI, and 1,700 walks. His 500th dinger was one of his 13 career walk-off home runs, the most in baseball history. Thome was elected in 2018.

JAMES HOWARD THOME
"JIM"
CLEVELAND, A.L. 1991-2002, 2011;
PHILADELPHIA, N.L. 2003-05, 2012;
CHICAGO, A.L. 2006-09; LOS ANGELES, N.L. 2009;
MINNESOTA, A.L. 2010-11; BALTIMORE, A.L. 2012

LEFTY SLUGGER POWERED HIS WAY THROUGH 22-YEAR MAJOR LEAGUE CAREER, AMASSING 612 HOME RUNS WITH A TEXTBOOK UPPERCUT SWING. AUTHORED SIX SEASONS OF AT LEAST 40 HOMERS AND 12 SEASONS WITH 30-OR-BETTER. DROVE IN 1,699 RUNS, INCLUDING NINE YEARS WITH 100-OR-MORE. DREW 1,747 WALKS, PACING THE A.L. THREE TIMES. LED CLEVELAND TO 1995 AND 1997 A.L. PENNANTS AS KEY MEMBER OF INDIANS RENAISSANCE. FIVE-TIME ALL-STAR FIRST BASEMAN BEGAN CAREER AT THIRD BASE. BECAME EIGHTH PLAYER TO TOP 600 HOME RUNS, REQUIRING THE SECOND-FEWEST AT-BATS TO DO SO.

JOSEPH PAUL TORRE

"JOE"

NEW YORK, N.L. 1977-81; ATLANTA, N.L. 1982-84;
ST. LOUIS, N.L. 1990-95; NEW YORK, A.L. 1996-2007;
LOS ANGELES, N.L. 2008-10

A BEACON OF SERENITY AND STATURE IN THE DUGOUT. WON
2,326 GAMES, FIFTH-MOST ALL-TIME. MANAGING IN FIVE
DECADES. LED YANKEES TO POST-SEASON IN EACH OF HIS 12
SEASONS AT THE HELM, WINNING 10 DIVISION TITLES, SIX A.L.
PENNANTS AND WORLD SERIES CROWNS IN 1996, 1998, 1999
AND 2000. ALSO PILOTED BRAVES TO POSTSEASON IN 1982 AND
DODGERS IN 2008-09. WON A.L. MANAGER OF THE YEAR AWARDS
IN 1996 AND 1998. IN 18 SEASONS AS A PLAYER, HIT .297 AS A
NINE-TIME ALL-STAR AND 1971 N.L. MOST VALUABLE PLAYER.

On July 18, 1940, Joseph Paul "Joe" Torre was born in Brooklyn, just a few miles away from Ebbets Field. Although Torre spent many days at the historic ballpark as a boy, he could not have imagined that nearly seven decades later, he would don a Dodgers uniform. His 18-season playing career began with the Milwaukee Braves in 1960, and Torre went on to be named to nine All-Star teams, win a Gold Glove in 1965, and was the 1971 National League MVP. His 29-season managerial career began in 1977 and finished in Los Angeles in 2010. On his first day as the Dodgers manager, the team celebrated its 50th anniversary in Los Angeles. Below are, from left to right, Carl Erskine, Sandy Koufax, Don Newcombe, Joe Torre, and Tommy Lasorda representing 60 years of Dodgers baseball. Torre was elected in 2014.

Frederick Stanley "Crime Dog" McGriff played for the following teams: Toronto AL, 1986–1990, San Diego NL, 1991–1993, Atlanta NL, 1993–1997, Tampa Bay AL, 1998–2001, 2004, Chicago NL, 2001–2002, and Los Angeles NL, 2003. A five-time All-Star amassed 493 home runs, the first player to lead both AL and NL in home runs, and hit 30 home runs for five teams. He was also the second player to hit 200 home runs in both leagues. McGriff won two pennants and a World Series with Atlanta. He was elected in 2023.

When the Twin Towers fell on September 11, 2001, Rachel Robinson and Dotty Reese were in a Manhattan meeting regarding the statue of their late husbands, commemorating Pee Wee Reese placing his arm around Jackie Robinson in 1947. Some question this event's veracity. Jackie knew better: "Pee Wee left his position . . . walked over to mine . . . he put his hand on my shoulder as if to say, 'Jackie Robinson . . . is worthy of being a member of this team.' " Rachel Robinson preferred a statue rendition of this photograph.

On June 19, 2022, Sandy Koufax joined Jackie Robinson in the Centerfield Concourse at Dodger Stadium. He spoke for 10 minutes and thanked 46 different people dating back to his youth. He opened by summoning the memory of Jackie Robinson: "Sixty-seven years ago, Jackie Robinson became my teammate and friend . . . sharing this space with him is one of the greatest honors of my life. . . . Jackie went out of his way to make me feel welcome, and I'll never forget his kindness." Invoking the memory of friends, teammates, coaches, and managers, he added, "My only regret is that so many of them are no longer with us, and I am unable to let them know how much I thank them and how much I appreciated them." In his 50th year as a hall of famer, Sandy Koufax joined Jackie Robinson in bronzed immortality, eternally appreciated not only by Dodger fans, but by baseball fans everywhere. (Above, Keith Birmingham; below, David Hickey.)

If Jackie Robinson is the founder of the civil rights movement, then Rachel Annetta Isum Robinson is its first lady. In 1996, she reflected on her life with Jackie: "I was given a mission, along with him, at a very early age. I was given a reason for living, many tasks to perform, many challenges that broadened and strengthened me. . . . When I look back, I think of myself as a very fortunate person. . . . We had to live that experience moment by moment . . . always looking ahead... moving forward." On July 19, 2022, Rachel turned 100 years old, and the Jackie Robinson Foundation, which she founded, began its 50th year. Marking the occasion, their son David said of his mother that she was "strengthened and made joyful by the thousands of young people the Jackie Robinson Foundation has impacted." The "ripples of new possibilities" continue, always "moving forward." (Right, Charles Gekler.)

JACKIE
He waited
In the whiteness of the afternoon sun;
Black man on green ground.
He waited
In the shadows and touched the hand of human history.
Black man on green ground.
He waited
In the silence of his tongue;
Black man on green ground,
He waited
In the path of words
Which broke his bounds;
Black man on green ground.
He waited
As few men have ever
Waited
And endured
Before a multitude as no man before.
To have conquered the white sun,
Blinding,
To have sailed the sun and ridden
Its joy in tears
And
In laughter.
To have ridden the white sun, blinding
And to be
Struck
Struck
Struck
By the rising
Of
Your
Own
Black
Sun
Your crown was white;
...and waited.

"There's not an American in this country free until every one of us is free."

Jackie Robinson
42

DISCOVER THOUSANDS OF LOCAL HISTORY BOOKS
FEATURING MILLIONS OF VINTAGE IMAGES

Arcadia Publishing, the leading local history publisher in the United States, is committed to making history accessible and meaningful through publishing books that celebrate and preserve the heritage of America's people and places.

Find more books like this at
www.arcadiapublishing.com

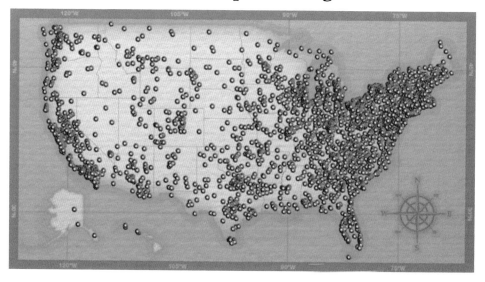

Search for your hometown history, your old stomping grounds, and even your favorite sports team.

Consistent with our mission to preserve history on a local level, this book was printed in South Carolina on American-made paper and manufactured entirely in the United States. Products carrying the accredited Forest Stewardship Council (FSC) label are printed on 100 percent FSC-certified paper.

MADE IN THE USA